Children In The Crossfire

Violence in the Home — How Does It Affect Our Children?

By Maria Roy

Health Communications, Inc.
Deerfield Beach, Florida

Maria Roy
Allentown, Pennsylvania

Library of Congress Cataloging-in-Publication Data

Roy, Maria.
  Children in the crossfire: understanding the effects of
spouse battering on children / by Maria Roy.
  p. cm.   ISBN 0-932194-71-0
    1. Family violence — United States. 2. Children of abused
wives — United States — Psychology. 3. Abused children —
United States —Psychology. 4. Children of abused wives —
Services for — United States. 5. Abused wives — Services for
— United States. 6. Women's shelters — United States. I.
Title.
HQ809.3.U5R68 1988   88-9454
362.8'2 — dc 19   CIP

© 1988 Maria Roy
ISBN 0-932194-71-0

Published by Health Communications, Inc.
          Enterprise Center
          3201 S.W. 15th Street
          Deerfield Beach, Florida 33442

Contents

Preface

Children across our country are struggling to survive the harmful effects of the violence they encounter in their own homes. They are the children whose parents are ravaged by the ill-effects of spouse battering. Their world is tragic, filled with uncertainty, pain and isolation. These children need help; they need it now. They need short-term intervention; but they also need remedial programs with long-range goals in order to stop the violence in generations to come.

This is a great challenge which we as a nation must face if we are to begin to reduce the level of violence both inside and outside our homes. At the present time, very little progress is being made in this direction. There are two basic reasons why. They are lack of money and lack of sympathy for the special problems facing battered women and their children. Granted, there is less tolerance for violence against wives now than there was even ten years ago. However, we need more financial and human resources in order to provide the specialized services for the children living in these circumstances. Shelters for battered women are usually understaffed and therefore lack the personnel to implement special services for children. Their budgets are austere and prohibit the establishment of any services other than meeting the critical need for immediate protection and refuge.

The personal, social and economic costs of violence in the home are astronomical. When the family is weakened by violence, society at large also suffers. There is a great financial cost to society which is reflected in federal, state and local budgets for human services and correctional justice programs focused on addressing "spin-off" problems, such as teenage pregnancy, juvenile delinquency, runaway adolescents and adult criminal behavior. Barnes and Teeters (1963)[1] in their book about criminology assert that criminals are molded by experiences that begin in early life. Violence in the home causes a great deal of turmoil for children. There is constant moving or shifting between relatives, frequent absences from school, isolation from neighbors. This transient and crisis-oriented lifestyle prevents the children from establishing roots, developing feelings of security and trust about grown-ups, or respect for their own self-worth. Abandoned emotionally and physically neglected and abused, they turn to a world of fantasy and often fall into a life of crime.

Roy and Caro (1981)[2] found that exposure to violence in the home during the formative childhood years produces aberrant behavior. Many battered women suffer from emotional breakdown and disengage themselves from their parental responsibilities. They cannot cope with what's happening to themselves and plunge into severe depression. One woman reported that her son was placed in a residential treatment center because he tried to hang the cat with a coat hanger and nearly choked his younger sister to death by sitting on her until her face turned blue.

Coker, Darrett and Gibson in an unpublished study (1979)[3] found that of the 135 men interviewed for the study, more than half reported that they felt their childhood experiences of disruption in the home were directly responsible for their incarceration. These men were convicted of three offenses of which at least two were crimes against the person defined as homicide, assault, sexual assault, robbery and kidnapping.

Efforts are being made to reduce the incidence of family violence in our society. In the meantime, the children need a great deal of support and encouragement. They need tailor-made services for their special needs and their only hope is the immediate response of the adult professional community which can advocate for the essential remedial programs in their local areas.

The purpose of the book is to provide a better understanding about the issues concerning spouse-battering and its impact on the children to encourage the creation of appropriate and innovative intervention programs. The book begins with a discussion of the underlying precipitators that contribute to the generational aspects involved in the self-perpetuating cycle of violence. The first three chapters show how our culture has tolerated and even condoned the use of physical force to resolve family conflicts. Chapter 2, in particular, demonstrates a reasonable estimation of the relative incidence of concurrent wife and child abuse. It concludes that child/spouse abuse represents a significant portion of the total universe of abused children per annum in the United States, a figure indicating a population of over 810 thousand children. Chapter 3 examines the psychosocial, psychiatric and historical causes of wife and child abuse, going one step beyond to uncover a third more fundamental common denominator referred to as the Cornerstone Theory of Family Violence.

The next section of the book presents a probing study of 146 children, ranging in age from 11 to 17 years of age. It is the first study of its kind which documents the intimate feelings, perceptions and concerns of children from violent homes. The key issues which surfaced during the interviews concerned physical and sexual abuse, psychological trauma, self-destructive coping mechanisms, assumption of parental or guardian role, educational neglect and poor school adjustment, auto-phobia, use and abuse of drugs and alcohol, peer paranoia, distrust of adults, unresolved conflicts and ambivalency about their parents, transition-induced stress, "accidental" victims of abuse, confused values, violence between teen couples and cynicism regarding their future.

Exploration of these issues revealed that wife-beating has serious and long-range effects on the children and puts them in a high risk category for physical and sexual abuse.

Next, the book delves into the dramatic and sometimes shocking details of children in a series of three individual in-depth interviews with young males and females who have lived the pain of incest and physical and psychological abuse. Their "individual portraits" paint disturbing detailed accounts of childhood turmoil and pain, bringing to life the myriad of problems uncovered in the study in the preceding chapter. The remainder of this section is devoted to interviews with adults who have their own perspective about the effects of wife-beating on the children.

The final chapter offers *concrete* help for wives, husbands and children caught in the *crossfire.* A listing of national sources of help and information is also included.

This book, in addition to being of interest to the general public, will also appeal to a diverse group of professionals who offer a wide variety of services to children in this category. They are students enrolled in courses about family violence, social work, child psychology; shelter personnel (volunteers, professional and paraprofessional staff); family doctors and public and mental health professionals; educators and researchers in colleges and universities and primary and secondary school staff (guidance counselors, school nurses, principals, school psychologists, classroom teachers).

In conclusion, if we are to reduce the impact of wife-battering on the children, several immediate steps have to be taken. Intervention requires the proliferation of crisis refuge centers, emergency shelters, safe homes, etc. Beyond meeting this primary fundamental need for safety and protection from physical harm, shelters for women and children should begin to develop strategies for providing extended and adjunct care to the families in need. This requires networking with existing community resources including pre-, primary, and secondary schools in the area. While most shelter programs are strapped financially, there are links in the community with family counselling services and parenting classes that can augment shelter services. Where services do not exist and there has been a demonstrated need for them, it is possible to approach high school boards to consider a proposal for hiring an on-site counselor (in addition to the guidance counselor) where young people can feel free and unthreatened to drop in for advice and direction about family and personal problems and drug problems.

In addition, family counselling services should develop programs for teenagers. Such services could use shelters as their primary referral source. The counselling processes should include:

1. Historical context of wife and child abuse
2. Analyzing the effects of sex-role stereotyping
3. Stress reduction and anger management
4. Non-violent conflict resolution
5. Accepting responsibility/violence avoidance
6. Exploring the consequences of violent behavior
7. Identifying and communicating feelings
8. Overcoming the hostage crisis (In cases of severe abuse, measures must be taken to address the child's victimization within the family in much the same way as one would approach counselling hostage victims who have survived life-threatening situations.)

Besides shelters, schools would also be a good referral source. Very often parents anonymous groups provide concurrent programs for the children. This offers an appropriate setting for implementing counselling services designed to modify violent behavior in adolescents from violent homes.

Providing counselling services for the teenage population is one of the greatest challenges for professionals because success relies on the provider's ability to:

1. Encourage the young person to agree to go for counselling.
2. Be committed to the goals and objectives of the counselling process.

Convincing the teenager that counselling is highly desirable is the crux of the matter. While many adults have a lot to lose if they don't change their negative behaviors, teens don't have nearly as much at stake, or so the situation is perceived by them. As a result, they may not approach counselling with a high degree of motivation for change. It would be extremely helpful for schools and shelters to launch student/resident information campaigns focused on understanding the consequences of violent behavior. This could be done through the normal curriculum or specified workshops and seminars. Courses such as civics, social issues, health, would be appropriate vehicles for presenting the social and legal consequences of violent behavior; this of course, with special emphasis on the ramifications of violence between family members and dating couples. Schools, in particular, should be addressing family violence in much the same way as they attempt to discourage chemical abuse.

Widespread campaigns about problem-solving approaches can have a positive effect on the student population and may eventually melt down individual resistance to changing negative behaviors. It would be worthwhile investigating offering "negotiation and conflict resolution" as elective courses for juniors and seniors in high school.

Next, it is extremely important for classroom teachers in all grade levels to be trained to settle disputes between children and assist the children utilizing various approaches to conflict resolution. Classroom teachers as a group could be the most influential role models for positive change if they become conversant with nonviolent problem-solving techniques and employ them on a day-to-day basis in the classroom. Improving listening skill, learning the art of participatory classroom management (quality circles of sharing and information), understanding the rewards of building self-esteem in the children through self-affirmation (self-confidence through encouragement), and creating a "feeling vocabulary" by encouraging the exchange of feelings around particular feeling themes, would produce an unthreatened positive environment for both academic learning and social interaction.

Acknowledgments

I wish to express my heartfelt appreciation to the following people who have helped me in my exploration of this study:

DiAnne Arbour of Jersey Women's Services, Inc., Morristown, New Jersey

Jean Arnold, librarian, Sinking Spring Library, Reading, Pennsylvania

Daniel T. Armstrong, Joseph M. Dell'Olio and Holly Grafton of CHILD, Inc., Wilmington, Delaware

Wallace H. Eckton, Jr., of AT&T Bell Laboratories in Reading, Pennsylvania

Thomas L. Lalley and James Breiling of the Center for Studies of Antisocial and Violent Behavior, National Insititute of Mental Health

Phyllis Paulson Sternlight of New Hope, Inc., Attleboro, Massachusetts

Barbara Purnell and Ruth Watson of the National Center on Child Abuse and Neglect, U.S. Children's Bureau, HHS, Washington, D.C.

Kendall A. TeSelle, Patricia LaRue and Sharon Ostrander of The Children's Home of Reading, Pennsylvania

Barbara Waldron of Alice Paul House, Cincinnati, Ohio

Grateful appreciation to my husband, Dr. P.K. Roy, for all his scientific and technical advice, in analyzing the data for Chapter 2, "Concurrent Child Abuse/Wife Abuse".

Special recognition must be given to The Cardinal Spellman Head Start Center, New York City, under the direction of Joanne Milano, where the impetus, energy and inspiration for the battered women's movement gained momentum and direction.

Dedication

To My Children, Milan, Jason and Michael
and To All Of The Children
Who Participated In This Endeavor

To the memory of Lisa Steinberg,
1981-1987, and to all the other children
caught in the crossfire.

Children begin by loving their parents. After a time they judge them. Rarely, if ever, do they forgive them.

Oscar Wilde
A Woman of No Importance, 1893

The Evolution of a Response

Exploring Resources, Providing Services, Heightening Public Awareness and Understanding the Scope of the Problem

> He abused me during the first pregnancy and my older son was born with a bruise down the right side of his head from a rifle butt that he hit me with one week before the delivery.
>
> (Anonymous in Roy and Caro's *Up From Battering*, 1981)

CHAPTER 1

Children from Violent Homes: The Larger Picture

When I first began to explore the problem of violence against wives, I was to a great extent unaware of its enormity and its complexity. I began my work by exploring services for battered women and discovered that in 1974 no specialized services for battered women existed in New York State. Further exploration revealed that New York was no different from other cities, both large and small in the United States of America. To my horror, I learned that battered women had no systematized network of help, and that institutions and society itself encouraged violence against wives by offering no legal or social recourse against it and no sympathy for the millions of victims ravaged by it.

Statewide Conference Points The Way

A statewide conference under the sponsorship of The Cardinal Spellman Head Start Center took place on the Lower

East Side of Manhattan on January 23, 1975. Victims and panelists were vocal in their shock and frustration. While official recognition of the plight of battered wives seemed essential, it was regarded by all as a long-range goal, one that could not possibly be realized in the short haul.

Panelists such as Marjory Fields, then a lawyer for the South Brooklyn Legal Service Corporation, Lieut. Mary L. Keefe, commander of the Police Department's Sex Crime Analysis Unit, and Carol Bellamy who was a State Senator at the time of the conference, offered information and suggestions for remediation along with Joanne Milano, Executive Director of The Cardinal Spellman Head Start Center. I organized the conference and as such served as panel moderator while carrying out my responsibilities as consulting social worker for the center. Feelings ran high as *CBS* local news and reporters for *The New York Times* recorded the myriad accounts of abuse which scores of victims shared with the audience.

Pleas for help resounded throughout the auditorium. Sometimes a whimpering woman giving testimony to her private hell at home would be embraced and comforted by another nearby victim. Other victims were more vociferous about their experiences and openly expressed anger about their situations. The day-long conference was an important milestone in the quest for needed legal, legislative and institutional reform that was to follow both in New York and in the nation at large. It was the beginning

Soon women were calling the Head Start office from Philadelphia, Newark and parts of Connecticut and even as far away as Florida. Media coverage exploded the problem through the local and eventually, the national networks. The phones were ringing off the hook in rapid fire succession. Head Start staff could not cope with the onslaught. Women were clamoring for help. They wanted it immediately. They needed it badly. The conference served as a validator of what heretofore had been a secret, private problem that nobody wanted to acknowledge or remediate.

No Place for Ostriches

The Cardinal Spellman Head Start Center became the first center in the nation to stick its head out of the sands of denial and open wide the need for crisis shelter and counselling. It served as a catalyst for the creation of the first specialized service for battered women and their children in New York State, where until as recently as 1966 beating did not constitute grounds for divorce. It became clear to Joanne Milano who headed up the Head Start Center and to me that we needed to explore the possibility of forming an independent non-profit organization to aid battered women and their children. Using the mailing list gleaned from the conference as a base to start contacting interested people, we scheduled weekly organizational meetings and before long Abused Women's Aid In Crisis, Inc. (AWAIC) was created. I was selected to serve as President and Executive Director. Naturally, I quit my job with Head Start and began the overwhelming task of securing funds, locating space, developing programs and building a paid staff comprised of a core of volunteers and student interns from neighboring colleges and universities.

What had started as a strictly voluntary limited telephone counselling service with monthly evening outreach meetings for battered women at Daytop Village (a drug rehabilitation program in midtown Manhattan) eventually became a full-fledged center of services, including telephone counselling and crisis intervention, individual and peer group supportive counselling, advocacy with clearinghouse function capability, outreach programs complete with speakers' bureau and a volunteer-training program for inhouse staffers and for outside agencies servicing battered women and their children.

Hyland Scesny, who was involved in the early pioneering efforts along with Carolyn Chrisman, a volunteer turned Director of Training and Volunteers, provided the steady flow of energy and optimism so sorely needed during those early days. Hyland offered spiritual guidance and philosophical insights which nourished my often faltering stamina. Carolyn on the other hand was extremely pragmatic about her contribution offering any and all services that she could possibly contribute. At one time Carolyn wore several hats in one day. She coordinated volunteers, provided telephone crisis counselling, acted as office manager and provided an educational workshop for a women's group in the city. Days like this were not unusual and until substantial financial support came, days like this were the norm.

The money did come. Nancy Castleman, a grants administrator for The Fund for The City of New York, responded to a proposal which I had sent her for "seed" money by meeting Joanne Milano and me. Not only was she successful in securing funds from her foundation, but she was also instrumental in opening the doors of many other city-based foundations. We were eventually able to service over 20,000 battered women and their children. In addition, we reached an even wider population by teaming up with larger more established institutions in the New York area. For instance, our affiliation with the Henry Street Settlement House enabled us to conjointly offer an innovative solution to the lack of shelter for battered women and children at a time when money for such matters was practically non-existent.

The Henry Street/AWAIC project became the city's first shelter to offer sanctuary to battered women and their children on February 17, 1977. It provided shelter for 32 individuals in 18 apartment units and offered counselling, education and recreation for the women and children. AWAIC provided a system of intake and referral to the shelter, a telephone hotline, monthly workshops and seminars. The marriage between AWAIC and the Henry Street Settlement was solidified as a result of months of planning with the City Council's Battered Women's Task Force and the Human Resources Administration. But this was not the only collaborative project. Empire State College of the State University of New York and AWAIC in conjunction with the State of New York, Department of Social Services, Office of Manpower Development entered into an agreement to provide a state-wide training program for New York State Local Departments of Social Service Employees. There were 14 major training populations served in the State including 12 different counties and two different New York City groups, over a two-year period. Russell Farnen served as Project Director of a staff of 15 professionals, 5 of whom were from AWAIC. Janice Montague served as AWAIC's Project Director.

Paula Weinberger, AWAIC's Director of Development and Program Expansion, was pivotal in co-designing the program with the Empire State staff. It was largely through her efforts that the joint effort materialized into the Domestic Violence Prevention Program and that both AWAIC and Empire State College were able to provide local social service workers with improved trainee skills for responding to victims in crisis situations; skill in identifying the battered family; knowledge of specific resources within the agency and for referrals; sensitivity to the background issues of domestic violence; capacity to profile families, batterers, couples; work group skills to select and use alternative counselling/treatment/prevention modes.

In the meantime, it became increasingly clear that there was a need for remedial programs for batterers. AWAIC, which had provided a full range of services to battered women and their children, launched a giant-sized outreach campaign in January, 1980, to reach men who batter. Men were encouraged to voluntarily contact specially trained counselors at AWAIC if they wanted to confront their own negative violent behavior and hopefully change it. The program which developed from the response to the campaign was geared towards self-referred males with a high degree of discomfort about the violence they were exhibiting toward their mates.

Details about the program and information for agencies desiring to replicate it in their own communities is documented in a recent publication of mine entitled *The Abusive Partner.*[4]

About the same time that AWAIC was offering services to self-referred batterers, it began a program at the Pre-Release Center of the Arthur Kill Correctional Facility in Staten Island, New York, for inmates in transition. This program was initiated by the Pre-Release Center's coordinating committee. The unstructured group model was the selected mode of intervention. It was designed to assist the inmates (about 85% of the inmate population at this facility have histories of violent crime, such as murder and rape) with reentry into their families. The goals of the program were manifold: to explore non-violent alternatives to spouse-battering, to inform inmates of the possible legal consequences for battering behavior, to identify sex-role patterns and their effects and to begin the process of self-awareness. The particular method and process along with case examples and implications for the future are also found in *The Abusive Partner*.[5]

Since 1975, AWAIC provided a myriad of programs and services including:

1. Counselling for victims of domestic violence, for men who batter and for children who witness battering
2. Public awareness campaigns
3. Professional and grassroots training and prevention programs, Advocacy for its clients and for the larger social issues, and Outreach and public education (including bilingual programs for the Hispanic community) through AWAIC's Domestic Violence Insititute.

AWAIC's counselling services were designed to meet the therapeutic needs of all members of the family experiencing domestic violence. This family approach was unique because it attempted to reach a wider number of clients than shelter facilities and other totally women-oriented agencies offered at the time. Individual and play therapy for children was innovative and quite unusual.

AWAIC was one of the first organizations in the nation to address the needs of abused women and their families. It was the first organization in New York City to offer comprehensive services to victims of domestic violence and has played an important advocacy and leadership role in bringing these problems to the public's attention. It organized its services around the following broad goals:

1. Providing a centralized service for abused women and their children, offering information, crisis intervention, counselling, and referral to appropriate agencies, organizations or shelters

2. Re-education and soliciting increased responsiveness on the part of agencies already serving victims of domestic violence, such as social service departments, the police, the courts and hospital emergency room staff

3. Promoting greater awareness of the problems of domestic violence on the part of legislators at the local, state, and national levels by participating on task forces, study groups or special panels to develop long-range policy goals which would encompass preventive and immediate services

4. Facilitating the creation of havens or shelters where abused women and their children can take refuge from life-threatening situations and receive the help they need in developing further options for themselves

5. Providing technical assistance and training to the staff of involved organizations

6. Fostering greater public awareness of the problems of domestic violence through use of media, publications, and frequent speaking engagements

7. Pooling and sharing information with other organizations and strengthening new organizations working on this problem

8. Developing programs to support abused women and their families in their efforts to become independent and to function successfully on their own

9. Intervening in patterns of violence passed from one generation to the next through therapeutic parent/ child programs

Agencies and shelter programs set up around the country cannot by themselves diminish the mortality rate of the many children of battered women who are killed behind the closed doors of their homes. In New York State where approximately 95,000 cases of child abuse are reported annually, 10,000 suffer serious harm and between 100 to 150 result in death. Almost 2,000 child abuse murders occur nationwide each year. These children fall through the cracks for a number of important reasons.

Elizabeth (Lisa) Steinberg's tragic death on November 5, 1987, which stunned the nation, is a case in point. She was only six years old at the time of her death. She suffered brain hemorrhage, extensive cuts and bruises of the head, back, legs and arms. Her death has been listed as a homicide. Her adoptive father, New York criminal trial lawyer, Joel Barnet Steinberg, was charged with the crime and held without bail. His companion of 17 years, Hedda Nussbaum, a writer and editor of children's books, who was treated for nine broken ribs, a broken jaw and nose and numerous other bruises believed to have been inflicted by Joel Steinberg at the time of Lisa's final beating, was also held accountable for Lisa's death for acting "in concert" with Steinberg and for endangering the welfare of a child.

New Yorkers demonstrated their outrage for Lisa's brutal death by enshrining the step outside her posh Greenwich Village walk-up on West 10th Street in Manhattan with bouquets of flowers. Her first grade class at P.S. 41 was gripped in sorrow at her loss.

We ask ourselves how this could have happened? Lisa Steinberg, like other children of battered women, was living in a highly volatile environment. Her mother, a seemingly unlikely victim of abuse, was reported by neighbors and colleagues from work to have been beaten on a regular basis for at least seven years. It may have even spanned a ten-year period according to some reports. Hedda had been hospitalized on several occasions for broken bones and in 1981 for a ruptured spleen. At no one time did she admit to the beatings, reach out for help or file a complaint with the police. Despite the fact that neighbors could hear her screams of torment and along with her fellow employees at work could see the bruises and scars, no one seemed to fear for Lisa's well-being or that of her 16-month-old adopted brother, Mitchell.

Some of the neighbors said that they complained to the police many times about Hedda's beatings. But a computer check showed that only one call was made during 1987. It was on October 6th. The police showed up — Hedda failed to press charges and police left the scene.

This case may not be typical of children of battered women because of the educational and professional backgrounds of the parents, and because she had been adopted (although there is a current investigation as to the legality of the circumstances of adoption), but there are many common threads which can help us to begin to see where and why the system failed and that it is symptomatic of larger problems.

There are many reasons why children of battered women are particularly vulnerable. Here are some of the more salient ones:

1. There is a misconception that child abuse occurs in isolation of other family problems. This is rare. Children of battered women are in a high risk zone. When an adult woman is living in a battering environment there is reason to suspect that the children in that household are in grave imminent danger; that they can be the victims of neglect and physical and emotional abuse.

2. There is a misconception that a battered woman can protect a child from physical abuse or that the child is in less danger because the woman is the primary target of abuse. Battered women are in no position to protect their children from being abused by their husbands or companions.

   Most battered women suffer from low self-esteem. After many years of physical and mental abuse, they become emotionally and economically dependent on their abusers. They may suffer personality changes and exhibit erratic behavior. Many become clinically depressed and require sedatives. Many lose their ability to love, nurture and protect. They may not even be able to make simple decisions concerning their own destiny.

Battered women lose hope. As a result of constant belittling they lose their self-confidence, self-determination and will to escape. In severe cases, where drugs and alcohol offer a way out, battered women lack the judgment and discrimination to care for the children in the household. More and more battered women are seeking help early on in the relationship so as to break the cycle of violence before it reaches this point. But when there has been a repeated pattern and history of abuse, there is reason to fear health and safety of the children.

3. There is a misconception that calling a child protective hot-line will result in an investigation and that the child's welfare will be protected. In actuality child protective services across the nation are hampered by huge turnover rates of case workers, large caseloads, late investigations, failure to identify high risk cases and failure to expunge unfounded reports.

4. There is a misconception that child protective workers are highly skilled, amply trained and heavily credentialed. Investigative casework is usually done by young graduates, who lack the experience and training to accomplish a most difficult job. Experienced social workers with MSW's rarely, if ever, are hired to investigate and follow-up reports of child abuse. And yet this work requires the wisdom of Solomon and the confidence of experience. Caseworkers are poorly paid and are being asked to enter highly dangerous situations that police officers are often reluctant to respond to. They don't carry guns, yet they may face a situation in which their lives may be threatened. Job dissatisfaction, fear of bodily harm and poor pay contribute to this national problem and unless these points are addressed, more children will continue to fall through the cracks.

It would make sense to hire experienced MSWs, offer financial incentives and professional and community recognition. In addition, revamping the practice of sending a helpless caseworker alone to investigate a report will do wonders. Teaming up with the local police precincts and dispatching a team, comprised of a plainclothesman with an experienced social worker could make all the difference in the world.

Also when reporting a case to child protective services, be prepared to follow-up on the call. Find out the person's name doing the initial intake. Call back to monitor what's been done. Be persistent. You don't have to identify yourself. If you feel that a child's life is in danger, don't drop the ball. Carry it as far as it will take you.

5. There is a misconception that the public at large doesn't bear the responsibility of seeking help for a victim of child abuse and that there is ample help being provided by departments of social services and private agencies. In reality one protective agency can't do the job. Relatives, friends, neighbors, are equally responsible for locating help for these children. Pay attention to the signs of abuse: unhappiness at school, marks and bruises, listlessness, crying when it's time to go home, disheveled clothes, poor attention span, clinging behavior, inappropriate adult-like behavior (children of battered women learn very early in life that they can't rely on the adults in the home for their survival. They often become the parents to their extremely needy mothers.)

6. There is a misconception that there is more help for children in middle class families and in homes with high income levels. The Steinberg case dispels this myth. While abuse may be less visible in these strata, there is no documented data to conclude that this group of battered children is at any less risk.

7. There is a misconception that the federal government is providing adequate funding for the welfare of battered children and more specifically, for the children of battered women. Actually there is an acute

need for increased federal spending for child abuse prevention and domestic counselling. Dr. Marcia Renwanz, Staff Director of the Subcommittee on Children, Families, Drugs and Alcohol of the United States Senate supports additional federal allocations.

As far as the private sector goes, many agencies such as AWAIC and shelters for battered women have suffered severe financial setbacks, requiring them to curtail or suspend direct services. There is a grave danger that the well will run dry for many more agencies nationwide.

A Vicious Cycle

Children growing up in homes where there is a high level of spouse-battering are in danger of becoming the next generation of batterers or victims of abuse. Children are impressionable; they imitate and repeat what is familiar to them. Children from violent homes are human time-bombs set to explode when they assume the role of husband or wife in adulthood. Most experts agree that violence begets violence and that it is passed on from one carefully taught generation to another. Many studies conducted over the past decade indicate that children who experience a high exposure to violence within the home coupled with low family warmth (hugging and verbal messages of caring and love) and a highly charged and stressful home environment are more likely to use physical punishment in their own families.[6]

One long-term study begun in 1956 involving 118 parents, 29 of whom had been abused as children and 89 had not been. The study concluded that:

1. Fathers who were abused as children were more likely to be abusive parents than were abused mothers (31% versus 19%).
2. About 41% of all abused subjects had children removed from their home by court action as opposed to 25% of non-abused subjects.[7]

It is worth noting that not all members of a particular family constellation become abusers merely because they were exposed to it in their family of origin. Some critics[8] of late of the generational theory of abuse point out that the learning theorists fail to explain why in a hypothetical family of four siblings where all have been exposed to violence, only one out of the four may actually exhibit violent and abusive behavior in their adult households. They contend that because three siblings do not go on to repeat the violence in their family backgrounds, the idea of generational transmission should be suspect and subject to more sophisticated research before any more claims can be made. While this caveat seems to be based on a sound logic, it is unrealistic to pose such a criticism because all social science theory, unlike physical scientific theories, are merely statistical trend analysis. Therefore, taking one or even a few isolated families in order to try to question the validity of the generational transmission of violence hypothesis, is unsound.

Agreed, more controlled research containing two statistically large groups — violent and non-violent is desirable to make statistically sounder predictions with minimum standard deviation. However, a recent survey conducted at Abused Women's Aid In Crisis, Inc., (AWAIC) based on 150 cases selected randomly from 1,000 cases, very strongly supports the generational cycle hypothesis. For example, 81.1%[9] of the abusive partners came from homes in which they themselves were beaten or where they had witnessed their own father abusing their mother. This demonstrates that there is a strong probability of generationally transmitted abuse with early exposure to violence. It does not explain why 100% of the abuser's siblings don't grow up to beat their wives and children but it does substantiate that when there is a high level of violence in the home, chances are four out of five that at least one sibling will tend to become an abusing marital partner and parent. This would confirm, rather than devalue the likelihood of the cyclic nature of spouse and child abuse.

One other point, when we refer to the transmission of violence as generational, we are not ascribing to the term the kind of certainty that would accompany a hereditary disease for example. What we are saying is that if we consider the home environment as tantamount to a school classroom, we could not posssibly expect all of the students (in the case of family violence the students being the children and the parents being the teachers) to learn everything that they observe or are taught in exactly the same way, nor do we expect all of the students will receive the same grades.

Battered Women/ Battered Children

Exploring the Relationship Between Matrimonial Violence and Child Abuse

All of these women (battered women) came to us for help and safety because they were in mortal fear of their lives. We take them in all hours of day or night with their cowering and frightened children.
(Joseph Dell'Olio, Executive Vice President of CHILD, Inc., Wilmington, Delaware, in *The News Journal*, Tuesday, Sept. 27, 1983)

CHAPTER 2

Concurrent Child Abuse/ Wife Abuse

It will be possible to attempt to demonstrate a reasonable estimation of the relative incidence of concurrent wife and child abuse by extrapolating figures from a combination of national studies and reports in conjunction with a study conducted at Abused Women's Aid In Crisis, Inc. (AWAIC).[10]

Methodology

Using data from an AWAIC survey with a data base of 150 subjects who were selected at random from among 1,000 of its clients (battered women), it will be possible to determine the relative coincidence of child abuse by applying the following formula: $N = 0.45N_W{}^*$ to estimates

---

*N= # of children who are concurrently battered with their abused mothers (N_W). The accuracy of the estimation of N from the empirical expression above depends solely on the accuracy of the determination of N_W, which has been reported to be about 1.8 million battered women per annum.[11]

derived from the National Study of the Incidence and Severity of Child Abuse and Neglect completed in December, 1980,[12] to the national survey conducted by the Family Violence Research Program at the University of New Hampshire over an eight-year period and published in 1980,[13] and to the Highlights of Official Child Neglect and Abuse Report (1983) conducted by the American Humane Association.[14]

The AWAIC study referred to above indicated that 45% of the assaults on the battered women were accompanied by similar physical assaults on at least one child in the household. The study did not include incidence figures of the number of battered women who also beat their children. There is no hard data on this population; only information via informal observation by staff at shelters for battered women. Shelter personnel commonly report that there is a high level of physical abuse of children by the battered women residing in shelters across the country. The problem is of such magnitude that most shelters have incorporated stringent rules barring the use of physical punishment as a disciplinary measure by mothers residing in the shelters. A growing number of shelters have offered workshops and courses in parenting without violence to help to alleviate the problem and to begin to make more long-term impact on level of violence in these families.

Utilizing the above formula, N is therefore equal to 810 thousand children who are beaten by either their mother's spouses or companions who are also wifebeaters. The actual number may be significantly higher because:

1. There are no statistics available for children who are beaten by their abused mothers.
2. The Family Violence Research Study (1980) excludes families with children under the age of three.
3. More than one child may be battered per family.

Discussion

The actual number should, therefore, be above the threshold value of 810 thousand children. However, there is no way of ascertaining a more accurate figure with present data as it stands. The Bureau of Justice Statistics Special Report on Family Violence states that statistical reports regarding the incidence of family violence reveal little more than estimates and that accurate statistical information is difficult to develop because of the following reasons:

1. Disagreement about defining the parameters of the problem, eg., when does spanking become an act of child abuse or a person's abusive behavior become criminal action or undesirable?
2. Disagreement about measuring the magnitude of the problem; there is a wide divergence of estimates because there are a variety of perspectives from which to study the problem, eg., social, moral, criminal justice and psychological.

What is important about the Report is the observation that the number of incidents of family violence reported by the Federal Bureau of Investigation's Uniform Crime Reports or the Bureau of Justice Statistics "cannot be considered as a measure of the true extent of the problem; rather, it highlights the seriousness of the problem of family violence if about 450,000 family violence victimizations are reported annually to a survey neither specifically designed for that purpose nor entirely adequate to that task."[15] The numbers will vary depending upon the focus of the study.

A study designed to determine the number of family members who are psychologically and emotionally affected by child abuse will most likely reveal a higher incidence of abuse than a study designed to measure criminal action. Similarly, a study aimed at developing statistical data about how families resolve conflict may result in much higher estimates about the incidence of violence than a study about the incidence of infanticide, patricide or spouse murder. The

National Crime Survey (NCS), sponsored by the Bureau of Justice Statistics, concludes "that during a nine-year period 4.1 million victimizations committed by relatives have been reported to a government agency (either the police, the Bureau of Justice Statistics, or both), and that a substantial number of these occurred at least three times during a six-month period," and should, therefore, be considered "a significant problem of large and currently ill-understood proportions."[16]

It is important to remember that most studies are just estimates of the truer and larger picture and that the truer picture is indeed a larger one. The reason for this is the underlying problem of under-reporting that occurs when attempting to measure the extent of family violence. The NCS suggests certain reasons for this: ". . . Many victims of family violence do not perceive their experiences as crimes. . . . Although interviewers are encouraged to interview each respondent privately, if possible, there may be other family members present during the survey interview. If the offender is present, the chances diminish that the victim would feel free to describe the event. . . . Many victims of family violence are reluctant to speak of their experiences because of the shame and revulsion they feel about the matter."[17]

Another interesting observation of the NCS concerns the characteristics of victims of family violence. Ninety-one percent of the spousal violent crimes reported to NCS were victimizations of women by their husbands or ex-husbands, who acted alone while committing the offense. Five percent were victimizations by wives or ex-wives alone; the remainder were primarily victimizations by a spouse or ex-spouse in concert with another offender.

This means that of the 259,000 crimes committed each year by spouses or ex-spouses, 91% or approximately 236,000 are perpetrated by husbands or ex-husbands against their wives and that nearly 13,000 assaults are committed by wives or ex-wives against their husbands. The Bureau of Justice Statistics Special Report on Family Violence does not ascertain the number of victims of spouse abuse per annum. What it does is estimate the number of victimizations or violent crimes reported by approximately 132,000 individuals who are interviewed each year. Likewise, when referring to the National Study of the Incidence and Severity of Child Abuse and Neglect,[18] it is important to remember that the estimates regarding child abuse and neglect derived from data collected from a sample of 26 U.S. counties located in 10 states are a "bare minimum number".[19] What makes this study unique and valuable is its consistent use of definitions at all data collection sites so as to reduce the margin of error.

The study reports that there are 652,000 abused and neglected children in the U.S. However, the actual incidence is considered to be substantially higher or at least 1 million each year.[20] Included in the definition of child abuse and neglect are the following subdivisions: Physical Abuse, Sexual Abuse, Emotional Abuse, Physical Neglect, Educational Neglect and Emotional Neglect. The total of all abused children in the study is 351,000. The total of all neglected children is 320,000. The AWAIC survey (above) reported the estimated percentage of wife batterers who physically abused at least one of their children at 45%. The National Incidence Study reports a total of 212,400 "in-scope" maltreated children (projected number of children meeting the study's definitions) who would have been known to local Child Protective Services (CPS).[21] It very aptly presents its data as an iceberg — the tip of the iceberg showing the 212,400 number of children. Scientific studies have indicated that floating icebergs reveal only one-tenth of their size. The tips of icebergs which float in the icy waters of the Arctic are really a fraction of their true size. Using the iceberg analogy and taking it one step further than the National Incidence Study, very likely, the actual number of maltreated children per year could be as high as 2.2 million children. In light of this projected figure, it is quite probable that 810 thousand children or 37% of the total number of abused children in the nation are from homes where concurrent wife or spouse abuse also occurs.

Conclusions

Concurrent child/spouse abuse represents a significant portion of the total universe of abused children per annum in the United States. The estimated projection of 810 thousand children residing in households where spouse abuse is also concurrent is predicated on the accuracy of the value of N_W which has been predetermined by a previous research project conducted by the Family Violence Research Program at the University of New Hampshire to be 1.8 million battered women. This figure has been commonly referenced by researchers and social service agencies, including police departments across the country, the U.S. Department of Justice, the National Coalition of Domestic Violence and many more.

Concurrent child/spouse abuse has always been known to exist. However, it has not been studied systematically except for the AWAIC study (1977) which indicated that "45% of the assaults on battered women were accompanied by similar physical assaults on at least one child in the household".[22] The above study takes the AWAIC study a step further and is pivotal in projecting the incidence of concurrent abuse nationwide. The empirical relationship $N=0.45N_W$ is valid in itself. The equation is valid regardless of the accuracy of N_W and can be very useful in the future when the estimation of N_W is determined with a greater level of confidence. To date the value of N_W is 1.8 million. It is possible that this number could change.

Considering that the American Humane Association for Protecting Children, Inc., in a recent report (1983)[23] indicates that "reporting levels (of child protective services) have increased 142% between 1976 and 1983" due to "vastly increased reporting".[24] It is quite probable that more and more of the tip of the iceberg will be revealed as increased documentation takes place by child protective services agencies in the United States. Unless something is done to break the cycle of violence of concurrent child/spouse abuse, our society will be faced with a runaway problem of infinite proportions. The number of children concurrently abused could be much higher than 810 thousand per year. In fact, similar to the growth of bacteria which multiplies rapidly, the incidence of concurrent child/spouse abuse could reach astronomical proportions in the very near future.

Getting Down to Basics:

Uncovering the Fundamental Cause of the Abuse of Women and Children

... the nation's ability to cope with the problem of family violence depends on knowing much more about how it is caused and what may be done to break the cycle of violence.

(Final Report of the *Attorney General's Task Force on Family Violence*, September, 1984)

CHAPTER 3

Child Abuse/Spouse Abuse: The Common Denominator

To date child abuse and spouse abuse have been considered as two separate social problems, each with their own set of causes and characteristics and each with their own corresponding solutions. For the most part there has been no attempt to view both problems as germinating from one root system or cause. Experts in each field of service or research have focused on their own area of concern, either child abuse or spouse abuse, and have rarely viewed each other's domain as congruent. Both psychosocial issues are relatively new ones and social action has evolved correspondingly as the champions of each cause develop direct services and prevention programs based on the most up-to-date understanding of what the underlying cause(s) may be.

Depending upon the investigator, different hypotheses suggest different causal factors. For instance, some experts feel strongly that psychopathology (psychoanalytic) is the ideologic precipitator, while others attribute the cause to psychosocial (social learning) shortcomings in the relationships between the abuser and the abused, and still others view it from a sociopolitical viewpoint. Below is a composite listing of some of the more common causes most often attributed to child abuse and spouse abuse.

COMMON CAUSES

CHILD ABUSE	SPOUSE ABUSE

I. PSYCHIATRIC DISORDERS

CHILD ABUSE	SPOUSE ABUSE
Hysteria	Masochism in wife
Schizoid personality traits	Paranoid schizophrenia
Character neurosis	Primary substance abuse
Depression	Depression
Narcissism	Obsessive-compulsive neurosis
Sado-masochism	Personality disorder
Poor self-image	Poor self-image
Dementia	Dementia
	Catathymic crisis
	Episodic discontrol

2. PSYCHOSOCIAL

CHILD ABUSE	SPOUSE ABUSE
History of family violence	Abuser's parental violence history
Poverty	Poverty/financial dependence of wife
Burdens of child care	Sex—role stereotyping
Early and unwanted pregnancy	Marriage on impulse or due to pregnancy
External stress	External stress
Media violence	Media violence
Isolation/mobile society	Isolation/mobile society

3. SOCIOPOLITICAL

CHILD ABUSE	SPOUSE ABUSE
Children as chattel	Women as husband's property
Customary extremes in discipline	Husband's right of chastisement
Rights of parents over children	Women as children/ patriarchal authority
Inequity of minor status	Sexual inequality

The above causes do not attempt to go beyond the symptomatology of child or spouse abuse. There is one step beyond symptomatology; a step which explains the fundamental root cause of both social problems. In a nutshell, it defines both the problems as growing out of the same soil. This is an important concept because it means that when we address the root cause we can begin to find the solutions for not just one of the problems, but for both of the problems simultaneously. Although this book does not investigate the abuse of the elderly, the discovery of the root cause for child and spouse abuse will also affect its solution as well.

There is a common thread, a common denominator which underscores most cases, if not all, of child and spouse abuse. The third group of causes (sociopolitical) leads to the discovery of the possible root cause. Notice that the sociopolitical etiologies for child abuse are quite similar to those for spouse abuse. It is from this group that the *Cornerstone Theory of Family Violence* emerges. Most experts agree that Group 1, (Psychiatric Disorders), is not a common cause of child or spouse abuse with the exception of primary substance abuse which accounts for approximately 51% of the abusive population. Usually when abusers suffer from primary psychiatric disorders, the concomitant negative behaviors are diffused to all aspects of one's life, activities and relationships and are not solely confined to the family. In other words, assaultive and menacing behavior will be a problem for the abuser, both inside and outside the family constellation.

Group 2, (Psychosocial), incorporates more effects or symptoms that are dedicated to abuse within the family and are less diffuse than the effects in Group 1. For instance, a history of family violence, burdens of child care, sex role stereotyping, unwanted pregnancy and financial dependence of wife have a bearing on the abuser's behavior within the home and very rarely carry over to situations outside the closed doors of the family.

In Group 3, (Sociopolitical), all of the effects on child and spouse abuse impact on the victims, and all of them are caused by worldwide sociopolitical ideologies which devalue children, women and old people. In other words, they arise from external political biases and institutional injustices, rather than from the microcosm of the family or pathology of the individual per se. This can best be understood in light of the documented history of violence against children and women. Below is a synopsis of the history of child and wife abuse. One can note startling similarities between the two historical summaries.

Historical Summary of Child Abuse

Helfer and Kempe in their landmark publication, *The Battered Child*,[25] include an essay by Samuel X. Radbill about the history of child abuse beginning with the ancient philosophers and biblical times spanning such cultures as the Greeks, Romans, Chinese, Crimean, American Indian, Arabian, Egyptians, Indian, Peruvian, Mexican, European, to name but a few. Dr. Radbill states that in ancient times infancy was the most dangerous time because in many cultures the child was not considered human until customary rites or ceremonies were performed. Traditionally throughout the world, the father literally owned the child and could sell it or kill it or abandon it with impunity. This meant that the child was the property of the father like his sheep or his bullock cart. Children as chattel were widely accepted. It was the prevailing world view. Children's rights and child welfare were unheard of at the time. Radbill specifies some of the rituals of the Athenians, Egyptians, Frisians and Romans.

For example, "In Athens the amphidroma ceremony was performed as a rule on the fifth day of life, when the new baby was carried by its nurse around the ancestral hearth to receive consecration and a name. If the child was not wanted, the father had to dispose of it before the amphidroma. In general, the longer a child was permitted to live, the more the parents became attached to him, and thus the longer he survived, the greater his chances for social recognition and parental care."[26]

Dr. Radbill cites many reasons for infanticide, eg., as a method of birth control in cultures that were ignorant of or lacking effective measures, or the shame and disgrace of illegitimacy, or when the mother for reasons of ill health or a host of myriad other reasons could not properly care for the child. Greed and with it various money-making schemes also led nurses and midwives and insurance brokers and burial clubs to infanticide.

It is absolutely shocking to discover that the murdering of infants was actually encouraged and permitted by the societies of the past and that infant children had no more rights than dogs, cats, poultry or cattle. Very often ritual sacrifice of infants took place to appease the gods for some natural calamity. In addition, they were committed in response to superstitions about curing disease, infertility and famine. All in all, infancy was an extremely perilous time, a time when the structure of society and its cultural more supported, justified, encouraged and perpetuated the murder of its infant children as an upright and socially responsible act.

Infanticide was the definitive premeditated act of murder that permeated a vast number of ancient societies. Next to infanticide child abandonment was responsible for numerous deaths of infants who were a burden to their parents. These babies would be left at prescribed "drop-off" places where they could be rescued by childless couples or sold off to slavery or beggarhood. It was not until 787 A.D. that the first foundling hospital was established by Datheus in Milan, Italy, and it was not until 1869 in New York City in the United States of America that the New York Foundling Asylum was instituted to care for abandoned and unwanted babies.

The road to improved treatment of infants and children has been a particularly arduous and tortuous one. Since ancient civilization slow steps to progress have been made.

The 20th century has achieved placing a man on the moon
and yet it is light years away from improving the plight of
children in modern societies. In the United States alone a
conservative estimate of deaths to children each year due to
child maltreatment is about 1,000.[27] Other forms of
maltreatment include physical abuse, sexual abuse, emotional abuse, physical neglect, educational neglect and
emotional neglect. The National Committee for Prevention
of Child Abuse (NCPCA) reports that over 2,000 children die
each year and that 1,000,000 American children suffer from
child abuse.[28] Obviously, it is a continuing problem of
significantly large proportion which has a long way to go
before it is conquered.

It wasn't until 1871 that the Society for the Prevention of
Cruelty to Children (SPCC) was founded in New York City.
It was established one year after the plight of poor Mary
Ellen Wilson, a beaten and neglected adopted child, who
came to the attention of a New York City church worker.
Despite attempts to have the child removed from her life-
threatening situation, the worker could not secure the help
of the police, nor the federal, state or local government.
Desperately she turned to Eldridge T. Gerry, an attorney for
the New York Society for the Prevention of Cruelty to
Animals.[29] He successfully championed the cause of Mary
Ellen Wilson and managed to secure a court order for her
removal from her abusive parents. Gerry, intent on
broadening the impact of the success of the Mary Ellen case,
then founded the New York Society for the Prevention of
Cruelty to Children. As a result of Gerry's pioneering efforts
and similar efforts in states across the country, child abuse
eventually became a crime in every state in the union.

It is deeply tragic to remind oneself that Mary Ellen was
rescued from the clutches of assaultive parents not because
she was a child whose life was on the brink of destruction,
but because Gerry based his argument on the premise that
she was a member of the animal kingdom, and as such
should therefore be entitled to the same protection afforded
to other members of the animal kingdom, such as dogs and

cats. If dogs and cats deserved to be treated humanely and protected from cruel and abusive environments, then surely Mary Ellen should be entitled to comparable treatment. It is quite sobering to keep this historical fact in mind when one is tempted to become impatient with the imperfections of the child welfare system of the 20th century. This is not to say that we should be cynical and apathetic because the problem is overwhelming. Rather, we should view the history as a documentation of a process towards progress which has been excruciatingly slow, but which is clearly an evolutionary one. Slightly more than one hundred years ago children had fewer rights and protection under the law than animals — a staggering piece of data and one that should stir both the mind and the heart.

It wasn't until the 1960s that the public cried out for battered children. This I attribute to the phenomenal electronic advances in communication. Television gained enormous popularity and stations were becoming more and more socially conscious. By 1960 more than 45 million households owned TVs in America. It was fast becoming America's favorite pastime. The '60s marked the turning point in the industry with the invention of the transistor at Bell Laboratories and represented the largest growth period in the number of homes with sets.[30] Television became the single most important instrument of information in our country and proceeded to instruct, inform and influence millions of Americans in a way that was unprecedented.

Pictures had enormous impact on our social and moral conscience. Concern about child welfare no longer remained an issue for academia or the professional case worker. Facts and figures were lifted off the dull pages of textbooks and reports and transformed into palatable forums as talk shows and news programs about child abuse were viewed by millions of Americans from all walks of life. Sitcoms during the '60s did not, however, reflect a realistic picture of disharmony in the home. The image projected by programs such as *The Partridge Family, Ozzie and Harriet,* or *Leave It to Beaver* was that American home life was stable,

loving and free of major crises. Drama during that era failed
to offer the public a balanced view of family life. It left out
the tragedy of child abuse which was ravaging the lives of
children behind the closed doors of their families.

It was during the '60s, 1966 to be exact, that Judge Warren
Burger ruled in favor of a petition filed by United Church of
Christ which was turned down by the FCC in 1964. In Judge
Warren's opinion, audience participation was necessary in
order to insure that the public interest in broadcasting be
represented. This meant that United Church of Christ was
allowed to actually participate in public hearings about the
license renewal of a television station in its community
(Jackson, Mississippi). This ruling led to the eventual
expanded participation of various community action groups
in broadcasting. All of these events helped to make
television more responsive to the health and social needs of
the community.[31] Public affairs programs became a standard
extension of the commercial networks and focused on
social and medical, as well as legal issues important to the
local and national community. Television's ability to reach
the masses at a time when public interest groups demanded
mandated participation in license renewal proceedings is
one of the chief reasons why the issue of child abuse and
neglect gained national attention. At this same time, the
federal government enacted additions to the Social Security
Act requiring the states to set aside funds for welfare services
and programs. In 1962 federal funds were appropriated to
assist states in this effort and to begin research into child
abuse and neglect.

The public could hardly ignore the growing menace of
child abuse and neglect. It was during the late '60s that
Doctors Kempe and Helfer shocked the nation with their
book *The Battered Child*.[32] Similarly, Dr. Vincent Fontana's
pioneering work with battered children at New York's
Foundling Hospital began to gain public attention. It wasn't
until the '70s that the public finally recognized child abuse
as a very serious social problem. The '60s had succeeded in
melting away public apathy born of ignorance about child

abuse. The '70s was the decade for state, federal and community and individual action. It marked a time when most states began to pass laws, not only encouraging doctors to report known cases to the authorities, but *requiring* them to do so.

Today, all states require physicans to report cases of child abuse to the state mandated agency where the child lives. Every state has a law against child abuse (each state's definition varies as there is not one consistent definition for all 50 states) which designates at least one central agency to receive and investigate reports of child abuse. In addition to physicans, dentists, nurses, teachers, social workers, foster parents, police and probation officers, family counselors and individuals who work directly with children are required by law to report suspicions of abuse of persons under the age of 18. However, we are relying on the good will and heightened sensitivity of the above professionals to report every suspected case. According to the American Association for Protecting Children, Inc., "Overall, reporting levels have increased 142% between 1976 and 1983, the only years for which this information is available . . . However, the rate of increase has declined over the years and remained relatively stable from 1980 through 1983."[33]

American law is based on English Common Law which placed a high priority on parental rights. It gave the father the absolute authority over his household and permitted him the right of total control over his children. He was allowed to discipline and rear them as he saw fit, even if he maimed or sold them in the process. Legislators on this side of the Atlantic did not deviate significantly from the legal traditions of their ancestors in England. During the 18th and 19th century America's lawmakers failed to pass laws for the protection and safety of children in the home. A man's children were still considered his property, and his parental right to rear his children according to his wishes included the right to abuse and neglect them as well.

It wasn't until January 31, 1974 that Congress enacted the *Child Abuse Prevention and Treatment Act*. The new law established the National Center on Child Abuse and Neglect which still exists today under the auspices of the Department of Health and Human Services. It was set up to provide training materials to states for the purpose of developing prevention programs and it was authorized to conduct research about abuse and neglect and disseminate information about the studies to all interested professionals or individuals working on the problem. The act also appropriated $85 million for these purposes to be spent over a four-year period (1974-1978). Private and individual efforts to assist abused and neglected children pre-dated the federal programs. For instance, the American Humane Association headquartered in Englewood, Colorado, was established in 1877 and Parents Anonymous was founded in 1970 by Jolly K., an abusive parent who herself was abused and neglected as a child spending the better part of her youth in over 35 foster homes.

Historical Summary of Wife Abuse

Just as British Common Law "legislated" the abuse of children, it also "governed" the abuse of women, particularly wives, and permitted husbands to beat their wives "with a rod no thicker than his thumb". This regulation was considered to be a lenient piece of legal reform benefiting wives whose husbands were previously allowed by law to use any reasonable instrument of chastisement. The history of the abuse of women and the subjugation of wives mirrors the history of abuse against children. Whether perpetrated here in the United States or abroad, the widespread abuse of wives was considered the right and privilege of the husband and was legally sanctioned. Women, like children, were the property of the family patriarch. Fathers owned their children; husbands owned their wives. The status of wives was no better than the status of their own children. Both wives and children shared the same unique position in the family. They possessed no legal status and lacked civil or criminal remedy against physical abuse and neglect.

The abuse of wives is not unique to the United States and England. It exists in cultures around the globe. Terry Davidson chronicles the long and devious history of the abuse of wives in *Battered Women: A Psychosociological Study of Domestic Violence.*[34] She probes the religious and political origins of abuse in Western cultures and traces the history from biblical times up to modern America. She answers her own queries about the possibility of raising public consciousness despite the ancient laws and the biblical injunctions and states: "Yes, there is reason for hope. The child abuse laws broke through similar barriers once the public became aware of the extent of the problem."[35] The Greco-Judeo-Christian heritage is one in which husbands traditionally exercised ultimate control over their wives. The 16th to 18th centuries marked times when wife-beating was permitted provided that it not exceed certain limits of abuse.

For instance, in 18th century France husbands were allowed to use their fists to punch and their feet to kick or thump on the back provided no permanent traces remained. They were not, however, permitted to use "sharp edged or crushing instruments,"[36] such as knives or axes. Provided the husband used *moderate* physical force against his wife, he could not and would not be subject to legal injunction. An accepted saying during the Napoleonic era was "Women, like walnut trees, should be beaten every day."

The Napoleonic Code influenced the laws of Belgium and Luxemburg, Holland, Switzerland, Italy and Germany and had even reached across the seas to affect the laws of Bolivia and Japan.[37] Napoleon disenfranchised women when he took over the reigns of government. "When Napoleon came to power, he imposed his views that women must be legal minors their entire lives. They were owned by their fathers first, and later, by their husbands."[38]

Champions of the cause were few and far between. In England the philosopher John Stuart Mill caused a furor of controversy with his sympathetic essay "The Subjection of Women" (1869). Prior to Mill's essay, an English clergyman,

William Heale, in 1609 published "An Apologie for Women, or An Opposition to Mr. Dr. G". His assertion, held in the Act at Oxforde Anno 1608 that it was lawful for husbands to beat their wives. Selected passages such as the one which appears below were translated into modern English by Quandra Prettyman Stadler and are found at the beginning of each chapter in Maria Roy's *Battered Women: A Psychoso-ciological Study of Domestic Violence.*

> Indeed some ancient ages of barbarism (before either civility was fully embraced or Christianity firmly established) seemed to draw from nature the practice of some such tyranny. Africanus reports of the Scythians, Tacitus of the Germans, Gellius of the Romans, Caesar of the French: with whom it was a received custom to dispose of their wives both life and liberty according to their pleasure. And hence it was that Mr. Doctor William Gager seemed to allege his history Publius Sepronius who divorced his wife for seeing a play. Of Ignatius Mecennius who beat his wife for being found in his cellar. Of Fannus who killed his wife for drinking a cup of wine. Fit proofs for confirmation of such a truth. Recount the time, it was in a paganistic and barbarous age. Observe the persons, they lived as mirrors of rigor and cruelty and are registered as monuments of murder and tyranny. Weigh the reasons that moved them thereunto; they will sooner call you into laughter than persuade you of imitation. Lastly judge of all and all is but as though a physician should go into an apothecary shop where is a variety of wholesome medicines, yet prescribes he some poison, some drug to strength his sick patient.[39]

Sir William Blackstone, on the other hand, chose to liken the status of women to those of children. In his *Commentaries on the Laws of England* (1765-1769),

Blackstone wrote ". . . the law thought it reasonable to intrust him (the husband) with this power of chastisement, in the same moderation that a man is allowed to correct his apprentices or children."[40] Blackstone's publication was to have an enormous effect on the legal status of wives in the United States of America.

In 1824, the state of Mississippi upheld the husband's moderate use of chastisement with impunity in order to preserve domestic order or in an emergency. In 1871, Alabama and Massachusetts revoked the ancient privilege of wife-beating, and in 1874 the North Carolina court rescinded the ancient rite as barbaric under any circumstances and made special reference to the accepted practice of flogging a wife with a rod no bigger than a stick as being reprehensible. In 1894 the Mississippi court overturned its previous legalization of chastisement. By 1910, 37 of the 48 states permitted wives to divorce on the grounds of extreme cruelty. However, because the law qualified the grounds as having to meet extreme or excessive definitions of what constituted cruelty, "moderate" cruelty was, thereby, implicitly allowed.

While some headway was being made regarding the institution of favorable legal reform, another important movement was gaining momentum. "The Women's Aid movement began in London in 1971 by Erin Pizzey, who held meetings with women who wanted to talk and share their concerns. Many of these women were desperately trying to find a refuge from an intolerable home situation. The Chiswick refuge, one of the first in the world, was founded in response to this need. There are refuges for women scattered throughout the world in Canada, Ireland, Scotland, Germany, New Zealand, etc., which indicates that wife-battering is a world-wide problem."[41]

Here in the United States of America similar concerns were being addressed. On February 2, 1975, J. C. Barden reported in an article appearing in *The New York Times* about a conference at The Cardinal Spellman Head Start Center located in lower Manhattan. "At a recent day-long conference on the abused wife, a panel of social workers, police officers, lawyers, politicians and a Family Court judge expressed the need to define the scope of the problems and discussed possible steps to alleviate them . . . Most of the vocal victims of wife abuse . . . had left in frustration by the time the conference ended in the late afternoon. But there were indications that their pleas for help had made an impression on some of the panelists."

Abused Women's Aid In Crisis, Inc. (AWAIC) was a concrete response to the voices of protest heard during that landmark conference in the United States.

"There were a handful of shelters in America; none of them publicized outside their own locality. AWAIC was the only agency devoted exclusively to helping battered wives." [42]

Shortly after the conference, AWAIC was founded as a private non-profit organization offering direct services free to battered women and their children while simultaneously implementing a training institute, a speaker's bureau and a clearinghouse function. A full-fledged public information campaign launched by AWAIC resulted in an onslaught of media interest. Most of the interest was of a sympathetic nature. Reporters from local and national networks were soon to devote segments of news coverage or total programs to the exploration of the issue. Magazines such as *Newsweek, U.S. News and World Report, Psychology Today, Parade,* to name a few, carried articles about the problem. *Ms. Magazine* did a cover story on it for its August, 1976 issue. Judith Gingold wrote the cover story entitled "One of These Days — Pow! Right in the Kisser", and I was asked by the magazine to promote the issue on a media tour arranged by the publicity firm Sheri Safran Associates which included an interview on the *Today Show,* UPI Audio Network in New York and the *Panorama Show* in Washington, D.C., in addition to various other radio and television shows.

The response to this kind of media exposure was extremely positive. Shelters and coalitions began to spring up around the country. Battered women as a group were going public for the first time in the history of our nation and this time their voices were not being ignored. The Crimes Against Women Tribunal (February 27-29, 1976) at Columbia University's School of International Affairs provided a forum for battered women and their supporters to testify openly. I spoke on behalf of the women who needed support services in the city, but who were too fearful to go public. The federal government began to demonstrate interest. In 1977 and 1978 I was invited by Rosalynn Carter, honorary chairperson of The President's Commission on Mental Health, to serve as a working member of the commission's Task Panel on Women.

On January 30-31, 1978, the United States Commission on Civil Rights sponsored a consultation under the chairmanship of Arthur S. Flemming to study the problems of battered women. I was also asked to serve as a participant at the Groves Conference on Marriage and Family at Airlee House, VA in 1978, and was invited as a featured speaker at DHEW, Office of Human Development Services' Conference about services to battered women, which was held at Colorado Women's College, Denver. The Carter Administration was committed to developing concrete programs at the federal level and implemented the Office on Domestic Violence in May, 1979, in the Department of Health and Human Services (HHS). It appropriated funds for a national clearinghouse, for state and local networking demonstration projects, for support of the Center for Women Policy Studies, for advocacy demonstration projects, for the development of public service announcements, for a national survey conducted by Louis Harris, Inc. in conjunction with funds from NIH and the Department of Defense, and for training materials to improve the sensitivity of judges and court personnel. Without further elaboration, many additional federal programs were initiated during this administration as some of the most prolific legislation in support of battered women's issues was enacted while Carter was in office.

However, support for federal assistance began to diminish before Carter left office. An attempt to streamline the federal budget led to a series of blows which nearly crippled the financial backbone of the battered women's movement in America.

The Law Enforcement Assistance Administration (LEAA) was the first federal program for battered women. It began in 1977 but because of budget cuts, it was phased out in the fall of 1980. In addition, Congress failed to approve domestic violence legislation during its lame-duck session in November, 1980.

After Carter's administration, the Office on Domestic Violence (ODV) was dismantled and closed in January, 1981. The Comprehensive Employment and Training Act (CETA), which often provided paid staff for shelters and job training for qualified individual battered women, lost its authorization in 1982.

Stiffer regulations and cutbacks in food stamps, public assistance, subsidized housing and employment training have made it more difficult for battered women to receive aid or to become self-sufficient and economically independent. Fortunately, recent passage in September, 1984 of a shelter amendment to the Child Abuse Prevention and Treatment Act, which was originally introduced in 1978 as the Family Violence Prevention and Services Act by Representative Barbara Mikulski (D-MD), will provide states with funding to local public agencies and non-profit organizations for technical assistance and training programs. It is administered by the Department of Health and Human Services over a three-year period. Similarly, the Department of Justice recently announced a national Family Violence Project awarding close to $300,000 for a two-year project against spouse abuse to the National Coalition Against Domestic Violence (NCADV). The National Coalition was organized at the U.S. Civil Rights Consultation in Washington, D.C. (1978). It is a grassroots membership organization made up of women and men who are working to eliminate family abuse. It is headquartered in Washington, D.C., and comprises approximately 700 shelters for battered women in 48 states.

Perusing through the above synopsis of child and wife abuse, it is impossible to avoid noticing the striking similarities regarding the origins of such practices. Both are pandemic "social diseases" germinating thousands of years ago in cultures and societies around the globe. R. Emerson Dobash and Russell Dobash remark in their recent study that . . . "The relationship between husbands and wives was once almost identical to that between parents and children. The husband's use of physical force against his wife was similarly an expression of the unequal status, authority and power of marital partners and was widely accepted as appropriate to the husband's superior position."[43] These similarities are the basis of what can be referred to as cornerstone for Unicausal. Both problems are a direct result of the age-old tradition of patriarchal ownership of wives and children, an historical fact and one which cannot be disputed. These traditions were entrenched in societies for centuries and their legacy, although somewhat less apparent today is certainly an underlying foundation for the conscious and unconscious 20th century prevailing attitudes which continue to undermine the struggle against child and wife abuse. While most societies today do not go so far as to condone infanticide or spouse murder, they still exercise a tolerance for various forms of abuse and neglect under certain circumstances and within specified parameters because they subscribe to the belief that family matters are personal matters — that the family is sacrosanct, and that crimes of violence against children and wives are somehow different and distinct from the same crimes perpetrated against strangers. Because these crimes are viewed as a *special category*, the legal response is based on the relationship between the victim and the abuser, rather than on the nature of the crime per se.

The Attorney General's Task Force on Family Violence sums up this idea in its Final Report (1984), "If a husband beats his wife or if parents abuse their children, this is a private matter. This view is still widely held by the public although decreasingly by some law enforcement officers, prosecutors and judges. Yet what reasonable person can learn of a battered child or woman, seriously injured or too often dead, and say that the government has no role to play in protecting individuals from other members of their families"?[44] That there was a need to express this view and to pose the impassioned question verifies how tenaciously our modern day society adheres to the ancient premise.

The Cornerstone Theory of Family Violence

Ever since the inception of the Cornerstone Theory of Family Violence, family violence has had but one cause: the patriarchal right of ownership of wives and children which has been entrenched in societies around the world. While the patriarchal right no longer exists in its extreme original form, modern societies around the globe are still strongly influenced by this legacy, but are in most cases unaware of the critical importance that it continues to have on the complicated inter-relationships within the family of the 20th century. All of the research which heretofore suggests that family violence has multiple causes, such as arguments over money, jealousy, sexual problems, alcohol, unplanned pregnancies, stress etc., are really attempting to describe the nucleating and contributing factors which are triggers of violent negative behaviors.[45] Such research falls short of identifying the one common underlying cause. If the common cause is eliminated or reduced, there will be a significant corresponding reduction in the incidence of family violence. Therefore, a massive public information and public education campaign, coupled with a corresponding relational, societal and political commitment to create an egalitarian society will have a direct effect on the level of family violence within that society.

Discussion

The Cornerstone Theory of Family Violence derives from the historical context of violence against wives and children, relying heavily on the similarities of origin, eg., the belief that wives and children were the property of husbands and fathers, respectively, thus leading to the concomitant societal tolerance and justification for the maltreatment of both groups. The theory assumes that the resultant societal policy and action led to the dehumanization of women and children and contributed to their common bondage. Wives and children as property devalued their worth as members of the human race and eliminated them from the protection of human rights.

There has been an evolutionary process of countering this unfortunate human condition. However, it has been centuries in the making. Today there is a conscious effort to improve the status of wives and the position of children in the family. A great deal has been accomplished in realizing this goal, but a great deal needs to be done. The theory implies that the Women's Movement and Child Welfare Movement cannot proceed on parallel tracks if we are to affect a systemic societal change. Both movements do have their specific agendas and this is legitimate and should definitely be preserved.

Obviously, women as adults require equality and equal protection afforded adults under the law. Children require the assistance of the adult community to protect their health and safety as minors. Aside from these specific differences, both movements would benefit from an essential relationship to the human rights movement. The rights of children (inside or outside the home) and the rights of wives (also women's rights in a much broader context) are part and parcel of what we should come to know as basic human rights.

It is important to keep in mind that the quest for equal legal status and equality for women is based on the desire of adult female individuals to gain control over their own destinies by claiming the rights and freedoms granted to adults in their society. Women are no longer legal minors in Western countries. However, women still need to achieve equality in the workplace, in politics, in the home and in the arts and sciences. For women to participate in designing and co-controlling their nation/world, they are to advance their argument from a human rights point of view because their emancipation is a question of justice and not one of social expediency. If society is to truly recognize the rights of women, it cannot avoid the issue of human rights. If women are to be "free at last", the social order requires that they be given the status of free, dignified, human beings and that all such beings be considered as "created equal".

The rights of children must also be argued from a human rights position. It serves no purpose to purport that children are entitled to protection under the law, yet because they are legal minors are not human beings and, therefore, should not be accorded the human rights of all dignified people who populate the nations of the world. The point is that men, women and children are the people who comprise society. It is no longer valid to rationalize discriminatory practices on the basis of sex (in the case of women) or on the basis of age (in the case of children). Children require a social and legal system which operates from this philosophical tenet. The fundamental precept is that children are complete human beings but undeveloped and immature adults. Because of this latter qualification, children's rights ought to be diligently guarded by the adult community. When children achieve adulthood, they are then expected to assume the duties and responsibilities of adults along with their civil rights. As adults they are no longer bound by the restriction of legal minors, but are charged with the obligations imposed on them by their society — obligations which flow from their newly acquired civil rights.

Human rights is synonymous with the total development of every human being. Another word for it is self-actualization or realized potential or self-cultivation or simply put, fulfillment. All human beings, all men, women and children, have the right to develop to their highest potential. When a society recognizes this fundamental human freedom, it cannot develop this social order into a system that contradicts the first order — human rights.

A society which concerns itself with the total development of each human member has no place in it for physical
abuse and neglect. In fact, the term abuse and neglect would
be contradictory in such a society. A society which
recognizes the prime importance of human rights for
everyone would have no practical use for the brutality of
force and the calamity of negligence. And yet societies, even
in modern times, still preach the gospel of self-determination, but invariably practice selective oppression. For
centuries women and children have been subjected to the
selective oppression of the patriarchal systems of the world
order. The barbaric treatment of women and children
originated from the world vision of women and children as
dehuman, that is, as undeserving of the dignity, value and
importance afforded the male population. For centuries
women and children have not enjoyed the freedom to
develop to their fullest potential as human beings. For
centuries women and children were bound by societies
which have defined them in terms of their husbands or
fathers, respectively. For centuries women and children
have been owned by their husbands and fathers respectively. Because they were owned, their status was no better
than that of animals or inanimate objects. Because they were
owned, they were not considered as human beings, but, first
and foremost, as property. Because their status as human
beings was non-existent, their maltreatment could be easily
tolerated and was, in fact, encouraged. Herein lies the basis
for the Cornerstone Theory of Family Violence. Herein lies
the erroneous justification for the maltreatment and abuse
of wives and children. Herein lies the common denominator from which wife and child abuse are derived. Herein lies
the common cause: the patriarchical right of ownership of
wives and children.

Conclusion

If wives and children are truly to be unoppressed and
unabused, the vestiges of political, societal and religious

ideological practices need to be examined in the light of human rights issues. The abuse of the elderly is also a direct effect of the right of ownership inherent in the patriarchal system. It is when the elderly lose their capacity to control their everyday lives, when they become economically or emotionally or physically dependent on their children that their status changes from adult to dependent. They become their children's children and are at high risk for maltreatment and abuse.

Below is a figure demonstrating the Cornerstone Theory of Family Violence and its relationship to the larger problem of debased human rights in general. The wider scope of human rights encompasses racism as well as sexism and ageism. The term ageism is broadened to include discrimination against children on the basis of age, although the word *ageism* is commonly used to describe discrimination against the elderly and does not usually refer to legal minors.

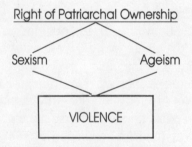

Figure 3.1. The Cornerstone Theory of Family Violence

Direct to Us from the Children

Probing the Minds and Hearts of the Most Vulnerable Victims of Spouse Abuse

When he'd (her father) plunge out of his chair to go over and hurt her, (her mother) I'd hurry between them, begging, "Please, Daddy, please don't . . ." In the emergency of the moment, I'd forget that I'd only be hurt myself. I just couldn't remain the non-reacting observer my father required. My little brother, on the other hand, was very good at watching without comment. When I tried to draw him into my plans for escape or rescue, I was met with little enthusiasm. It puzzled me then. Now I realize he might have been petrified.

(Terry Davidson in *Conjugal Crime*, 1978)

CHAPTER 4

Silent Witnesses Speak Out:

A Study about the Intimate Feelings, Perceptions and Concerns of Children from Violent Homes

This study is based on a sample of 146 American children ranging in age from 11 to 17 who were identified by professionals (educators, social workers, mental health counselors and therapists and psychologists) as children who came from homes in which wife-beating was a major problem. All of the children during the course of the study were not living at home. The majority were residing in shelters with their mothers; the next largest group were in group homes or protective homes for children. The smallest group were living at a friend's or relative's home. All of the children were selected for the in-depth interviews because of their verbal communication skills, and their willingness to speak openly about their experiences in a confidential setting.

Methodology

The study was conducted over a 36-month period. Interviews were pre-arranged by obtaining clearance from agency or program directors, and in the cases where children were living with friends or relatives, permission was given by a parent (usually the mother) or a custodial guardian. All interviews were face to face and supplemented by file case histories whenever this was possible and permitted. All subjects were coded to insure anonymity. The subjects were identified by professionals who were either working with them at the time of the study or who had had previous contact working with them. Criteria for identification was based on the children's exposure to high levels of violence in families of origin and where wife abuse was documented or highly suspected. In cases where the children were residing in protective homes for children or in group home settings, a series of two to three pre-selective group meetings were held with the identified subjects in order to discuss their feelings about participating in the study; to describe the purpose of the study and the research process; and to ascertain whether or not the subjects met the established criteria of: having a background of family violence (wife-beating), being reasonably comfortable participating in in-depth individual interviews and possessing good verbal communication skills. In cases where the preliminary group interviews could not be arranged or were not possible because the setting (private home) did not allow it, preliminary individual screening interviews were scheduled to determine subject eligibility.

During the screening process 297 subjects were interviewed. However, 97 of the children were screened out of the study because they did not perceive wife-beating to be a serious problem at home and because there was not enough documentation in their case histories to contradict their perceptions. The remaining 54 children either declined to commit to the research process or having once committed, reneged early on and withdrew voluntarily from the study. Others were not able to complete the study because they were removed from protective custody and placed in alternate facilities or returned to their homes or placed in foster homes where continued contact could not be established.

The sample size is limited and the study is exploratory, making the findings somewhat tentative. There is another drawback to the study since it was not possible to interview more than one sibling in each family, where there was more than one child in the family because siblings were either too young or too disturbed, or because they were in another facility or in the custodial care of an adult residing far away. However, there are a number of elements that are common to each child's experience. These elements are key factors in determining the effects that wife-beating has on the children who witness it. These key factors are:

1. Physical and sexual abuse and neglect
2. Psychological trauma
3. Self-destructive coping mechanisms
4. Assumption of parental or guardian role
5. Educational neglect/poor school adjustment
6. Auto-phobia
7. Drug use — an escape route
8. Peer paranoia (stigma complex)
9. Distrusting of adults
10. Unresolved conflicts and ambivalency about their parents
11. Transition induced stress
12. Frequent "accidental" victims of assault
13. Confused values
14. Identification crisis
15. Evidence of perpetuation of cycle in teen couples
16. Cynicism about their own future

It is also worthy to note that while the children were able to respond reasonably intelligibly and with logical sequence to the questions posed during the in-depth interviews, none of the children exhibited superior verbal skills. Generally speaking, they tended to use grammatically correct structure speckled with occasional slang expressions and the vocabulary was repetitive and limited although by no means significantly sub-standard.

Of the 146 subjects, the majority interviewed were females. There were 93 girls and 53 boys. Some of the shelters did not allow teenage boys or boys over the age of 15 to accompany their mothers and siblings. Many boys tended to be less interested in participating in the study and were usually perceived by the professionals as less skilled or less bent on expressing their feelings.

Although the sample is biased because of its small sample size, it does contain representative cross sections of the population ranging from rural to urban dwellers; to multi-ethnic and multi-racial, such as whites, hispanic and blacks, (Asian, Middle-Easterners and Native American populations were not sampled); to a cross section of socio-economic classes (lower, middle and upper). Not all the respondents answered all of the questions, particularly those questions which required reflection or self-perception. Usually their response would reflect uncertainty about expressing an opinion or a perception. This produced varying numbers responding to information about highly speculative or highly subjective aspects of their experience. For the most part, the correlations and cross-correlations of the key factors are based on the sample size.

Key Factors

A. Physical and Sexual Abuse and Neglect

Case history reports and subject responses indicate that 48% of the population had been physically abused by either parent but that the father was the primary abuser in most instances (90% of the time during the period when the family was intact and living together as a whole) and that the mother was usually perceived by the subjects as unable to cope with the wife-beating and thus negligent of her parental responsibilities. Once the mother and the children left the abusive home, the mother became the primary disciplinarian and tended in 85% of the cases to become abusive both verbally and physically and was described by many children as impatient and a "screamer".

Twenty-eight percent of the females reported that they were sexually abused by their fathers. None of the male subjects reported incidents of sexual abuse and there was no information in their case histories to negate their responses. Of the females reporting problems of sexual abuse, 10% were documented cases with child protective services involved. None of the girls was in individual therapy; four were in group counselling sessions provided on site at their shelter residences. The girls revealing the sexual abuse ranged in age from about 13 years to 17 years. Another three percent of the females in the study had case histories of documented sexual abuse, but did not verbally attest to this. All of them were below the age of 12.

The physical abuse was described by the subjects as a serious pattern of assaults which were most often concurrent with incidents of wife-beating, but which were not exclusive to the wife-beating. These assaults involved being beaten with straps, baseball bats, electric cable, as well as with the bare fists. In five cases the children reported that they were pursued by their fathers with a loaded gun. After a beating, one girl hid in a corn field overnight with her younger sister in order to avoid being shot to death by her enraged father. One boy revealed that his mother who was seemingly described as depressed and withdrawn held a loaded pistol to his head for a five-hour period. He said that he believed that she would have killed herself and him had it not been for the timely intervention of a case worker from Child Protective Services who had a scheduled visit on that day. He was literally "saved by the bell". His mother, despondent over her near suicide/murder attempt, confessed what had been occurring and turned herself over to mental health authorities. The boy was removed from the home and placed in a home for children.

Forty-one percent of the children felt that their fathers had a drinking problem, that their dad was most abusive during a drinking bout, but that there were times when the abuse occurred when there was no apparent consumption of alcohol. Eight percent of the group indicated that their dads smoked pot and two percent believed that other more potent drugs were involved. Twenty-four percent of the children felt that their mothers abused alcohol to "forget the beatings". One teenager who was also sexually abused by her father described her mother as being heavily sedated most the time. At one time she remembers her father smashing her mother's head through the plasterboard in the kitchen. This girl also revealed that an older but emotionally fragile sister who was also continually molested by her father had recently given birth to his baby and that this baby was living with her sister and mother at home in constant danger of repetitive abuse. The subject was removed from the home when she voluntarily told a school guidance counselor that she wanted to leave home and needed help. The girl was subsequently placed in a foster home.

All of the males who were 15 years and older stated that they tried to protect their mothers from being beaten by intervening during the assaults. One boy warded his father off with a broken soda pop bottle. Another boy used a bread knife, while another picked up a lamp and actually threw it. Most of the time the boys attempted to use their fists or shoving. One boy wrestled his father to the floor but could not overpower him. He sustained a dislocated shoulder and had several front teeth knocked down his throat. They did not consistently intervene physically. It usually occurred once or twice, and in 87% of the cases immediately preceded the mother's decision to leave the abusive home.

About 50% of the younger males (ranging in age from 11 to 14) said that they had fantasies about fighting back and that they would retaliate when they got bigger and stronger. The remainder felt that they would never be able to physically challenge their fathers.

While none of the girls fought back by direct physical confrontation, 10% of them harbored morbid fantasies in which a tragic event, such as a car accident or a heart attack or suicide or overdose of alcohol or drugs might provide the solution to the problem. These thoughts were usually expressed as wishes on the part of the girls. One girl went so far as to pray every night that her father would "die in his sleep". Another girl acted out her fantasy of death by fire when she set her home on fire and jeopardized the lives of the entire family including her own.

B. Psychological Trauma

All of the children indicated during the course of the interviews that they were pained by their father's violence against their mothers or themselves. While they did not use the word "pain" to describe what they were feeling, their body language indicated to a great extent that recollections of the violence in the family was very disturbing to them. Some of them experienced "lumps in their throats" while remembering particularly unpleasant events. One boy kept picking at a sore on his arm. One girl blinked excessively. Many of the girls looked mature beyond their years, using excessive makeup and puffing on cigarettes. Many implied by revelation of their behavior that they needed nurturance. Two of the girls interviewed revealed that they were prostituting their bodies because as one of them put it, "I feel good knowing that I can be attractive to men and that they need me."

Most of the teens were seriously involved with a steady boyfriend or girlfriend. Even the girls who were active in prostitution had steady male partners. One of them was romantically involved with her pimp, who was at least 20 years her senior.

Ninety percent of the teens were sexually active (this was true for all of the girls who had been sexually abused by their fathers. All of these girls had boyfriends they were planning to marry some day.) The steady partners of the subjects were described as runaways, prostitutes, alcohol and drug abusers or school dropouts. Some even indicated that they had boyfriends who were serving time for drug trafficking, armed robbery, felonious assault, pimping and drunken driving. The most common problems ascribed by the boys in the study to their girlfriends were running away from home, abusing drugs and dropping out of school.

Sixty percent of the boys in the study frequently got into trouble with school authorities because of rowdiness and open hostility to teachers and peers. Chronic truancy rounded out the picture. The truancy was the precursor of dropping out of school and then finally running away from home.

An astounding number of children (including the preteens) revealed drug and alcohol dependency. Eighty-five percent of the subjects said that they had been drinking since they were eleven; two percent said they started as early as nine years of age.

Feelings, such as guilt, shame and fear, were also expressed and will be discussed as specific key factors below. Four percent of the population stated that they had nightmares when they were living at home, but that the problem diminished and completely disappeared when they were removed from or left the abusive home.

Ten percent stated that at the time of the interview they were continuing to have bedwetting problems, which plagued them as far back as they could remember. This was a constant source of embarrassment to them, especially since they were living in fish bowls at shelters and homes for children. Many of them suffered from chronic insomnia because they tried to stay awake all night, rather than be caught wetting their beds. One boy said that he pretended to go to sleep and then when everyone was alseep he'd sit up in bed and read comic books with the aid of a flashlight.

All of the children had received some form of crisis counselling/peer group or group counselling upon admittance to a shelter for battered women. However, those who had never taken up residence in such a facility or who were referred to larger custodial institutions did not receive such services. While some of the children were being seen for individual psychological counselling at facilities outside of the residences, most were not. None of the children were undergoing therapy or receiving counselling which directly addressed the problem of overcoming their own aggressive/ hostile/violent prone behavior. In spite of the overwhelming need for such services, there were no community or shelter-based counselling services or programs for preteens and teenagers to assist them in regulating their negative behaviors and to help them to learn how to monitor their unwanted behaviors and then reprogram their behavior pattern on a non-violent track.

C. Self-Destructive Coping Mechanisms

Some of the self-destructive strategies for coping with violence in the home have been alluded to above. For instance, the problem with anger, hostility, aggression and violence that many of the male children sustained, in particular, could be viewed as undesirable coping mechanisms. Other acting out behaviors included truancy, running away from home and prostitution. The children tended to view these approaches as positive solutions to a chaotic family life. They felt that these behaviors were self-preserving.

"You see," indicated one 14-year-old boy, "I ran away from home because I hated what was happening, and I wanted to get away from the fights between my mom and dad. I didn't want any part of it. Even if it meant starving or stealing to stay alive, it was better than staying home and watching the beatings."

The other forms of escapism were also seen as a way out of an intolerable situation. The prostitution was perceived as a positive step towards independence and "security". The girls in the study who chose this escape mechanism thought that through it they had been initiated into the rite of adulthood and took pride in the fact that they could earn money and live in an adult world. Entry into this world of adult men and money seemed a great deal safer than the hopeless world of the child in the homes from which they

were running away. These girls said that they found true
love and that their pimps, although tough and sometimes
rough with them, "really cared" about them. They were, it
seems, trading one form of abusive situation for another.
The tragedy is that they did not see the parallels in the
situations and were not cognizant of the real physical danger
and psychological harm that they were placing themselves in.

Interestingly enough, most subjects (both male and
female) stated that their friends were having similar
problems at home and that they didn't socialize with
"straight" kids. Theirs was a world of brawls and verbal
assaults and they naturally gravitated toward young people
with similar problems. They found comfort in knowing that
other kids had private hells at home. It was for them a
perverse form of group therapy. There was solace in
confirming the brutality of their harried lives; other kids
were hurting and so the misery of their company diminished the pain of being different. It was a form of
rationalization for the destruction that they, themselves,
were imposing on their immediate lives. They were able to
accept their own violence because they were accepting it in
their choice of friends. On the surface they "needed" to be
perceived as tough and rugged rebels; underneath they
confided that they had fears about their developing violent
lifestyles. These fears will be specifically amplified in the
ongoing exposition of common experiences.

One of the 15-year-old girls had been picked up at
different times for shoplifting, truancy, possession of
marijuana. As with prostitution, crime represented a form of
power. In other words, it was an expression of control over
one's otherwise impotent and powerless life as a child.
Though destructive as a choice, it was viewed by the child as
a survival mechanism. This, of course, is paradoxical, but it
does appear as a common thread throughout case history
after case history.

Liberation from the bonds of a destructive, barren and
despairingly violent home life meant doing something
immediate with little thought about the long-range

consequences of their actions and with disregard for their own future. What mattered most to the youngsters who were *acting out* by *getting out* was whether they could actually physically remove themselves from the abusive situation. They wanted the abuse to stop — this was their primary concern. If it was not within their power to achieve this while they were living at home, they perceived that they had no other choice but to extricate themselves from the home and to take their chances. Many of these children said that as young children (ten years of age and under) they had fantasized about leaving home and had promised themselves that by the time they were in high school, they'd be able to run away. The *dream* of running away played an important role in their lives when they were in grade school. It was their salvation, so to speak, and it gave them a direction — something to *strive* for. It was for them *hope*. The healthy wish for a better life was realized in the complex self-destructive acts of emancipation. Crime, truancy, drug abuse and drug dealing, and prostitution were attempts to break away from a family system that seemed to pose a greater threat to their health and well-being than the romantic dream of escape and *living happily ever after*.

D. Assumption of Parental or Guardian Role

About 10% of the population indicated that they tried to protect their mothers from being beaten at one time or another. It usually occurred when they thought that their mother's life was on the line or when they felt personally responsible for the altercation between their parents. Both males and females comprised this group with the males dominating. The other females in the group who assumed a parental role did not do so by physical intervention, but by taking care of the household when the mother's coping mechanism dysfunctioned. They cooked, shopped, bathed younger siblings, did the laundry and assumed the normal everyday responsibilities of the parent. One girl stayed out of school for a two-week period in order to nurse her mom back to health after a beating which left her depressed and physically bruised. A black eye and lacerated eyebrow confined the woman to the home as she was in no frame of mind to have to explain her situation to neighbors or friends. These youngsters very often felt overwhelmed by their circumstances, but had no alternative other than becoming the nursemaids and caretakers of their households. A significant number of the boys opted for the role of abuser. About 20% of the boys (including some of the boys who at one time or another intervened to protect the mother) joined their fathers in victimizing their mothers. They identified with the aggressor and ultimately became the aggressors — a role they both loathed and admired.

What occurs in these situations is similar to the dynamics of a hostage situation, in which hostages (usually on an unconscious level) learn to accept their plight by minimizing the criminal acts of their captors and by rationalizing their inhumane behavior. The captors who represent power and authority, serve as a model for the hostages who desire to emulate their abductors and become powerful and authoritarian like them. Becoming the aggressor was a sure way out of the hostage trap. It meant taking sides and putting aside or burying any feelings of hostility and animosity that they harbored against their father's violent behavior. It meant again that they were striving for entry into the adult world and that fighting side by side with the aggressor insured a definite place in the patriarchal order of things. It is these violent-bound young boys who by internalizing the abusive male behavior become the *perpetual assault machines,* which churn out the cycle of violence generation after generation.

The females, on the other hand, rarely identified with their fathers. They tended to be more passive in their resistance to the violence in the home. In addition to becoming little *homemakers,* they became victim-oriented, silent, withdrawn and fearful of becoming the direct object of physical abuse. Those who were sexually abused submitted to the victimization out of fear of reprisals. These females were forced to assume the role of an adult female at an early age. They did not, however, feel that the sexual role imposed on them by their fathers emancipated them from the hostage trap in the same way that the abuser role tended to liberate the young boys. The imposed sexual role further enslaved them to a family system that exploited females and children.

The females in the study were in a double bind. Not only were they exploited because they were children, there was a double whammy because they were also females, which meant that there were even fewer roads out of the hostage trap and certainly no guarantees that once out, they would no longer be victims of abuse. These young girls were future wives and mothers, who had tasted all the bitter herbs that a violent home life could provide. They were more conflicted about what lay ahead of them. One part of them yearned for escapism of the romantic true love and the happy home of the future, while reality reminded them of their mother's miserable position in the family and their possible fate as similar victims of wife-beating.

E. Educational Neglect/Poor School Adjustment

The sample investigated had enormous difficulties in school. As alluded to above, these children were truants and dropouts. While in the lower grades, they were frequently absent from school due to the mother's injuries or to injuries they, themselves, had suffered. The war-like atmosphere at home was not conducive to studying. It created an immense distraction from studies and interfered with homework. School seemed to not be a priority for these youngsters. For most it was "kidstuff" compared to the harsh, sometimes life and death circumstances at home.

Of course, there are always exceptions to the rule. About 20% of the population were planning to complete high school. About half of these thought that they would go on to college. The bulk of the children were suffering from educational neglect. Many had reading and learning disabilities and were one to two grades below their chronological age. This was determined by case histories and in a few instances, by conversations with educational specialists who were involved with some of the children.

Those children with drug problems had little value for school, other than as a contact point for accessing substances, such as marijuana and methamphetamines (speed). The majority who were alcohol dependent (85%) were too often sleeping off hangovers or too sick to concentrate on the three R's.

Because of the alcohol and because of the identification with the aggressor syndrome many of the male teenagers exhibited poor impulse control by frequently losing their temper, at times becoming explosive and erupting into physical fist fights with other students at school. It was not uncommon for these boys to be fighting over a girlfriend. Some of them managed to become, not surprisingly, abusive with their girlfriends.

One boy said that he had punched his girl in the face, torn her blouse and thrown her books all over the lunchroom when he overheard her making a date with another boy from school. He was obviously suspended from school and was faced with civil and criminal charges brought against him by the girl's parents.

All in all, most of the children did not perceive school as a potential for positive change in their circumstances. In other words, they did not seem to value an education as a possible vehicle for improving their lives sometime in the future. The children were more interested in immediate solutions to their problems at home. School did not offer them prompt relief. The drugs that they could secure while at school would, however, give them the instantaneous brief respite from physical and mental anguish.

Another difficulty the children experienced was in relating to school authorities (teaching staff and administrative staff).

On April 19, 1977 (Ingram vs. Wright), the Supreme Court ruled to uphold corporal punishment in the schools. Teachers in loco parentis may "exercise powers of control, restraint, discipline, and correction as necessary, provided that the discipline is reasonable"[46] and under certain circumstances in accordance with the Supreme Court ruling. School, to these children, represents an extension of the autocratic vicious family system they are all too familiar with. One girl stated that she hated all the teachers because "they don't care and only want to mess me up by getting me into trouble." This mistrust of school personnel was rather common to most of the respondents. To fight a family system that inflicted both physical and mental pain was one thing, but to fight the tyranny that they perceived to be systemic in the schools was quite another. They would rather tune out and drop out than take on the system. To them it was the only solution. There was rarely a "significant other", such as a teacher or guidance counselor whom the children felt they could trust to talk to about their problems at home. Only one child, a female, indicated that she sought out the help of her high school guidance counselor. This girl was sexually abused by her father. She approached the guidance counselor after deciding that she needed the assistance of an adult to remove her from her home. This was accomplished and the girl was eventually placed in a foster home subsequent to her placement in a group home setting.

The difficulties described above tended to be typical — the norm for the respondents. There is little doubt after interviewing them that they were disenchanted with school, that school did not play a significant role in their everyday lives other than to serve as a drug distribution center, and that school for them signified a macrocosm of their abusive and violent homes.

F. Auto-Phobia

The term *auto-phobia* is used here to connote fear of one-self. About 95% of the respondents revealed that they harbored fears about their own behavior and what they could be capable of doing to themselves or to a family member (usually the father) if the circumstances became totally intolerable. *Totally intolerable* meant for these

children that conditions in the home either directly
threatened their lives, or the lives of their mothers or
younger siblings. Simply stated, these children were afraid
of themselves. They were terrified of the possibility that they
might commit murder or suicide or both. While the boys
feared that they could be driven to murder, the girls tended
to be suicide prone. Five percent of the female respondents
actually did attempt suicide (slitting wrists, drug overdoses).
While the males felt that they could be pushed to take their
father's life, no one actually committed murder. All of the
boys over 15 years of age managed to physically confront
their fathers at least once. Many of them revealed that they
were certain that they could go all the way if they were not
self-vigilant, if they didn't leave home, if their mother did
not leave, and/or if they stopped "doing drugs".

There was an alarming degree of self-doubt. "I'm not sure
what I would have done if we didn't get out when we did,"
confided one boy. "It wouldn't have been good to stay. I
know that because I almost broke his (father's) neck before
we took off," he continued. Another boy divulged that since
he was "bigger than my dad and I can knock him out if I want
to," he stayed out of his way as much as he could. He felt that
he could even "put him away permanently" if necessary. This
mistrust of their own reactions to the violence in the home
eroded their self-confidence and self-esteem. It did not seem
possible that these young people could in their short years be
so tortured and so troubled by such monumental fears.
Certainly the idea of parricide or self-imposed death must
have had a profoundly troubling and crippling effect on them.

This information is disturbing in the light of what Dr.
Robert Sadoff, Clinical Professor of Psychiatry at the
University of Pennsylvania and an expert on parricide,
revealed as a recent guest on the *Donahue Show* which
explored the issue of parricide. He stated that there is almost
a familial linkage between the abusing father and his own
victimization as an abused child, which is important to keep
in mind in order to reduce the problem from one generation to the other.[47]

Dr. Sadoff revealed during the same appearance that there are recognizable signs of imminent parricide in sexually and physically abused people. He stated that some of these indicators are personality change, eating and sleeping problems, homework problems, school failure, no friends, mood fluctuations and depression.[48] In light of Dr. Sadoff's expert opinion, the potential for parricide in the population of children from violent homes is extremely great. Most of the children who were interviewed for this study have met Dr. Sadoff's criteria for committing parricide. It is essential to understand Dr. Sadoff's observation that parricide is not something that happens just immediately, but occurs after repeated traumas over a long period of time. The person tries different ways of handling it, but finally feels so frustrated that he/she capitulates against a brick wall, believing that there is no way out of the situation. Finally, feeling trapped, the person kills the abuser to escape further entrapment.[49]

The children who participated in the study were children who had endured years of wife and child abuse in their homes. There was a definite pattern of abuse which was established over a period of years during their childhood. The environment for possible parricide is consonant with Dr. Sadoff's description of the kind of trauma experienced by children who actually kill a parent. Many of the children in this study complained about feeling helpless and unable to stop the violence in their homes. This common impression of impotence — of being incapable of improving the circumstances at home, of alleviating the anxiety or of attenuating the frequency and intensity of the physical abuse created a feeling of utter hopelessness and frustration. It was for them the "brick wall" which Dr. Sadoff so aptly alludes to.

This "brick wall" phenomenon is quite similiar to the chronic feeling of powerlessness that battered women describe when recounting feelings about their own victimization. Lenore Walker identifies these feelings of persistent helplessness in relationships with men as a type of *learned helplessness.* She bases her assumptions on the research of an experimental psychologist, Martin Seligman, who demonstrated that dogs confined to cages and subjected to random electrical shocks which were administered at unpredictable intervals eventually became so compliant, passive and submissive that when the researchers attempted to alter this procedure by teaching the dogs that they could escape over to the other side of the cage, the dogs still would not respond. Even when the door was left unlocked and the dogs were actually shown the way out, they continued to remain passive and refused to leave, thus reexposing themselves to shock.[50] Walker reasons that the theory of learned helplessness occurring when a subject is convinced that there is nothing that he or she can do to alter his or her circumstances, improve the situation or bring about a favorable outcome, applies to battered women. She comments that repeated batterings, like electrical shocks, reduce the woman's motivation to respond by making her become passive. She does not believe her response will produce desirable results and, therefore, does not believe anything she does will alter any outcome.[51] Dr. Walker's research has led her to believe there is a "high probability" that battered women who remain in abusive situations in which the abuse escalates will because of the learned helplessness syndrome "eventually be killed by or kill their own men."[52]

Faith McNulty's true story, *The Burning Bed,* describes the marriage of Francine and Mickey Hughes, which ended tragically when Francine who had been battered and abused during the course of their 13 years of marriage together, set fire to Mickey's bed while he was asleep on it. During that period together, Francine had been severely beaten and had come to believe that her life was in real physical danger. She suffered physical and emotional pain and had attempted to extricate herself on many occasions. Mickey's threats had a paralyzing effect on her. He is quoted in the book as having said, "Don't think you can leave me, you bitch. Not ever! You ain't *ever* gonna get rid of me! I'll find you wherever you go,

and when I do, it won't be pretty. I'll kill you inch by inch."[53]
She found herself breaking down both physically and
psychologically. She began to experience feelings of nausea,
rapid pulse, dizziness and suffocation. She avoided going
out of the house and being seen in public because she felt
ugly, stupid and unattractive.

Things worsened and she contemplated suicide. She
feared that she would have a nervous breakdown and go
insane. The random and varied frequency of abuse which
was ever increasing in frequency and severity made Francine
lose sight of the possibility of escaping. She saw no light at
the end of the tunnel. When she poured gasoline around the
bed where her husband lay sleeping, she firmly believed
that in killing him she and her four small children, Christy,
Jimmy, Nicole and Dana, would be spared from death. She
perceived his death as her only alternative. If she and the
children were to survive, then Mickey had to die.

During the trial Dr. Anne Seiden, staff psychiatrist at
Michael Reese Hospital in Chicago, testified on Francine's
behalf. Dr. Seiden felt that at the moment when Francine
surrendered to her husband's beating on March 9, 1977, and
was forced to endure numerous indignities such as "when
she crouched in the corner of the kitchen with garbage
smeared in her hair and told Mickey she wouldn't go to
school anymore"[54] (Mickey ripped up all of her school
books from the classes she was taking at Lansing Business
College in Michigan and ordered her to burn them), she
became acutely psychotic and was unable to keep her
impulses under control due to ego fragmentation. This was
the culmination of the dreaded day when Mickey beat her
and degraded her. It was that final act of capitulation that
triggered her to permanently remove him and his threat to
her and the children.

Francine Hughes killed her husband because he subjected her to repeated beatings over the 13 years of their
marriage and because she felt that her life and the lives of
her children would eventually be taken by him. She did not
believe at the time she killed her husband that she had any

other alternative. She killed Mickey Hughes in an attempt to control her life and extricate herself and her children from the ultimate fate of death. All her attempts to free herself from his domination had failed. Francine was affected by the syndrome of learned helplessness. When she became convinced that she and her children were in imminent danger of death, and that the only resolution to this problem was in his death, she acted in an attempt to save her and her children from such a fate.

The Francine Hughes' case demonstrates the tragic consequences of violence in the home. The children who live in these violent homes are also in Dr. Sadoff's opinion capable of killing the person they perceive to be a physcial threat to themselves. The children who were interviewed for this study were acutely aware of this possibility for themselves. Their greatest fear was in knowing that they had the potential to kill their father — the thought had crossed their minds. They had even fantasized about how it would happen. This acknowledgment added to their feelings of helplessness and despair. It was for them a hopeless cycle of autophobia reinforced by the continuous physical abuse to which they were subjected.

Since it is rather complicated to predict violent behavior, it would be prudent to avoid generalizing whether a certain group of individuals (in this case children from violent homes) is any more prone to violence than children in the general population without the benefit of controlled research. Psychologist John Monahan in his book *Predicting Violent Behavior* indicates that one of the most important questions to ask in prediction is, "What is the person's history of violent behavior?" He cites five indices of violence: (a) arrests and convictions for violent crimes; (b) juvenile court involvement for violent acts; (c) mental hospitalizations for 'dangerous' behavior; (d) violence in the home, such as spouse and child abuse; and (e) other self-reported violent behavior such as bar fights, fights in school, arson, violent highway disputes, and perhaps violence toward animals."[55] His major concern is in ascertaining whether or not an offender has a potential for future criminal violence. However, one can apply his research findings to the population of children in this study by posing and attempting to answer some of the same poignant questions that Monahan asks in determining an offender's capacity for repeated acts of violence. Monahan queries:

1. **What are the person's relevant demographic characteristics?**

   The children in the study are pre-teen and teenagers under the age of 18. *(Studies indicate that violence peaks in the teens and early 20s.)* Over 85% of the population were alcohol and/or drug dependent. *(Drugs tend to increase the probability of violent behavior, particularly alcohol which inhibits one's ability to contain anger and rage.)* Most of the children in the study had low academic achievement. *(The less education, the higher the likelihood of violence.)*

2. **What is the person's history for violent behavior?**

   All of the children in the study come from homes in which there is a high level of violence between the parents and in many cases between one or both parents and one or more of the children in the home including the subjects. These children were exposed to violence over a sustained period of time which usually extended over the duration of their childhood. All of the males in the study who were over the age of 15 had used physical force against their fathers in an attempt to protect their mothers during a beating. Fifty percent of the younger males fantasized about fighting back at a future time when they would be physically able to succeed. Ten percent of the girls hoped for a violent resolution to the abusive situation at home and five percent of the girls had attempted a self-inflicted form of violence, suicide. Sixty percent of the boys in the study were frequently involved in violent confrontations with teachers and peers at school. Ninety-five percent of the population indicated that they felt that they could be driven to parricide or suicide or both if the right set of circumstances were present. They felt that this violent resolution of their problem at home was inevitable if they continued to remain within the home under the control of the abusive parent. The fear of the possible consequences (their own death, incarceration, institutionalization) did not play a critical role in assessing their options and alternatives.

3. **What is the base rate of violent behavior among individuals of this person's background?**

Monahan reiterates throughout his book the importance of the base rate of violence and emphasizes that it is the most significant information in making a prediction.[56] The base rate is the frequency with which violence is committed in a given period within a particular group. There are at present no base rates for the specific population of children in this study, ie., there are no frequency rates of violence for children who come from homes where there is wife-beating, nor are there rates for adults who grew up in such violent homes. It would be valuable to know these statistics. Such information would be critical to developing intervention and prevention programs and would, no doubt, help to establish the relative impact of wife-beating on the national crime rate, on the rate of parricide in this country and on the suicide rate.

The data reported in Roy's study (1977)[57] show that 81.1% of abusive partners had experienced a high level of wife and child abuse. The base rate of wife-beating in a population of adults who witnessed wife-beating as children must be significantly high.

Strauss, Gelles and Steinmetz in their book *Behind Closed Doors: Violence in the American Family*[58] measured family violence with a technique that was developed at the University of New Hampshire in 1971, which is known as the *Conflict Tactics Scale*. The Violence Scale indicated annual incidence rates of violence per 100 over a 12-month period. However, there was no way of determining the age range of the group of respondents who were reflected in the child-to-father and child-to-mother rates and whether or not the children were also exclusively from homes with a wife-beating problem.

4. **What are the sources of stress in the person's current environment?**

The children in the study feel powerless about changing their violent home situation. They were fearful of being abused, both physically and in some cases sexually. They were afraid that their abusive parent might severely injure, permanently maim or kill the abused parent. Most of them have a problem with drugs and alcohol. Many of them were overwhelmed by the assumption of the parental role.

5. **What cognitive and affective factors indicate that the person may be predisposed to cope with stress in a violent manner?**

About 95% of the children in the study believed that they could in event of intolerable life-threatening circumstances kill their abusive parent and perhaps do physical harm to themselves. Many of them had already been involved in at least one violent confrontation with their abusive parent. Many revealed that they had an active fantasy life depicting themselves as murdering their abusive parent or of killing themselves. Many expressed their own self-doubt about being able to control this tendency towards parricide and suicide.

6. **What cognitive and affective factors indicate that the person may be predisposed to cope with stress in a non-violent manner?**

The children in the study did not demonstrate strong tendencies to inhibit their violent inclinations. They did not focus on the legal or emotional consequences of parricide and were, therefore, in a constant state of arousal. Their safety valve was in hoping and in some cases planning to extricate themselves from the violent home by running away or by accompanying their mother to a refuge center. Basically they were dependent on an external control mechanism, rather than an internal one.

7. **How similar are the contexts in which the person has used violent coping mechanisms in the past to the contexts in which the person likely will function in the future?**

The assaults on the abusive parent usually occurred while the children had attempted to intervene during a violent confrontation between parents for the most part. The older boys fell into this category. They indicated that as they grew in stature and as the arguments between parents intensified and occurred more frequently, there was a greater risk for more violent responses from them.

8. **How are the likely victims available to them?**

They are readily accessible since they are residing in the same household.

9. **What means does the person possess to commit violence?**

In the case of parricide, the child would have access to the same means available to the abusing parent: kitchen knives, furniture, gasoline for fire and in some cases firearms. Also as the boys grow in stature, they become physical equals to their fathers. The girls who committed suicide have easy access to drugs and knives and razor blades in the home.

Monahan's set of questions (above) have relevancy for the population of children in the study and help to clarify any doubts or questions concerning the tendency of the respondents in the study to commit parricide or suicide. Having answered the nine critical questions of predictable violence, it appears that adolescents who live in homes where there is a high level of violence between the parents are at risk of utilizing desperate means of overcoming the problem if they are not extricated from the violent home before a *totally intolerable* episode of violence occurs between the parents.

G. Drug Use — An Escape Route

Drug use in this population is widespread. The use of alcohol in 85% of the population started as early as age eleven. Two percent started at age nine. Over 50% of the population had used marijuana or methamphetamines; 10% were habitual users. They used drugs and alcohol because they were available and a relatively inexpensive means to, in their opinion, gain self-respect with peers, feel good and take the edge off having to face violence between their parents.

Drugs were perceived as a buffering agent. They provided a momentary escape route out of the real violence in the home. They were the magic genies in the bottles and "joints". None of the children indicated a desire to curb or stop drug use. To them it was a ready-made panacea and they were not going to relinquish their escape route out of hell. Powers and Kutash in their article, "Alcohol, Drugs, and Partner Abuse," state that "Multiple drug use abuse is a major problem. The use of different substances in combination or in sequence has become common, and the interactive effects of the substances may be greater than their effects individually . . . The use of multiple substances increases the difficulty of gauging the psychoactive effects . . . Unfamiliar or unexpected psychoactive effects may create panic reactions leading to reactive aggression."[59]

Powers and Kutash also warn that the combination of alcohol and amphetamines is particularly dangerous. They explain that substances may not produce the desired effects of escaping the violence in the home. Rather, they may aggravate the conflicts at home and reduce a person's ability to cope with the disharmony. Ironically substance use can amplify the level of violence in the home by increasing a person's use of violence as a problem-solving technique. The children who are turning to substances for temporary relief are decreasing the likelihood of experimenting with the use of non-violent solutions to their problems at home.

H. Peer Paranoia (Stigma Complex)

Adolescents (age 15+) tend to look to each other for social approval and recognition. What their peer group thinks of them is a major motivating factor during this period of enormous growth. As a group they avoid behaviors with a high risk of rejection and are known to take extraordinary risks in securing peer endorsement. For these reasons, adolescents in households with concurrent child/ wife abuse are very sensitive about the family secret which they try to keep hidden from the general population of their peers. They are subject to similar feelings of guilt and shame that so often afflict their battered mothers.

Betty Riley (fictitious name given to an actual battered wife in Roy and Caro)[60] stated, "I really felt this tremendous sense of shame and guilt about being in this situation (battered wife) . . . It was strange to live my life with a huge chunk in the closet, and to always have a secret."[61]

Adolescents as a group try to avoid situations which make them appear odd or different from their peers. The adolescents in the study revealed fears that their peers (especially at school) would detect their problem at home and use it to ostracize or ridicule them. The majority of the adolescents in the study tended to isolate their families from their peers. The fear of disclosure impelled many of them to participate in social activities occurring away from the home. Rarely, if ever, would they consider entertaining their peers within their homes.

One girl said, "You could never tell when something would set him (her father) off. So I felt it was better to meet my friends at the movies or the mall instead of at home. I didn't want them to see him when he got angry. They might be afraid and not hang around with me anymore."

While on the surface it seemed a rather positive and inventive way of coping with the fear of being detected, there was a negative side to it. The fear prevented most of the adolescents from voluntarily revealing the "hidden secret" to adults who might be in a position to offer assistance.

The females in the study tended to confide in one trusted friend more than the males. This was found to be consonant with Youniss' and Smollar's findings that," for most females discussions of intimate issues, such as feelings and problems, appear to be as much an aspect of their close friendships as are discussions of non-intimate issues. While this description is valid for some of the close male friendships, for many others, the exchange of intimate information is apparently not an aspect of the relationship."[62] Similarly, the males in this study usually avoided all discussion of family violence with friends and were more likely to minimize it or totally deny it. In general, for both male and female adolescents in the study it was a *taboo* subject.

I. Distrusting of Adults

Adults across the board were not to be trusted. They were not viewed as allies, but regarded with suspicion and disdain. The foundation for trust obviously was shaky, to say the least. The children in the study did not convey trust in their parents and projected these feelings of distrust and anxiety onto all other adults, such as teachers, other adult relatives and counselors.

The children responded negatively to such questions as:

1. Do you believe that your father will stop drinking and go to counselling?
2. Do you believe that your mother can be counted on to stop the violence?
3. Do you believe that your parents will go for marriage counselling?
4. Do you feel that your parents really care about you and what happens to you?

5. Do you feel that you can confide in your father/ mother?
6. Are there any relatives other than your parents who you feel you can trust? (The usual response was, "Yes," when referring to another sibling or an older cousin and, "No," when referring to an aunt, uncle or grandparent.)
7. Is there anyone at school, such as a teacher or a guidance counselor, whom you can talk to about your problem?
8. If yes, have you ever tried contacting them and talking to them about your family problem?

The factor of unpredictability was pivotal. The majority of children (80%) in the study had suffered through chronic periods of instability marked by moving in and out of their homes, moving to different locations (in some cases out of state), temporarily staying with relatives (in some cases with friends), seeking refuge at shelters for battered women, being placed in foster care and in a few cases detention centers. This constant shifting of location — changing home base — creates adjustment problems, which tend to result in anxiety and stress. This vicious cycle of upheaval-anxiety-stress triggers feelings of anger and resentment, which in turn produces a lack of faith and trust in their parents who, in their opinion, created all the chaos in the first place.

One boy said it all when he queried, "Why should I trust somebody who choked my mom, sent her to the hospital with broken ribs and beats me up whenever he feels like it?"

Another boy remarked, "I don't think nothin's gonna change anymore because nothin' has. We've moved a lot of times and we'll move agin'. I know we will. Nothin' ever changes." Note the paradox in the latter comment, "Nothin' ever changes." The boy is aware of the futility of changing their physical location, so much so that he does not regard his mother's effort to move out of the home as a sign of change. What he experiences in the continuous shifting from place to place is a constant state of flux that leads back to square one. One is reminded of the dog chasing its tail. There is seemingly a lot of activity. The dog makes quite a bit of flurry, it gets agitated, runs round and round, but it doesn't catch its tail after all, and even if it did, what difference would it make? The realization that they cannot rely on the good will and good sense of their parents is at the basis of their mistrust.

They feel betrayed and cheated. One girl said, "Forget it" when asked if she thought that her father could be trusted to control his temper once angered. "My father goes crazy when he's mad. He always yells a lot and nothin' nobody says or does stops him. When he gets started, *watch out.*" She added when asked whether or not she felt that other kids her age trusted their parents, "Other kids don't have fathers like mine. It's not fair."

The issue of trust came up when the children were asked if they knew of anyone other than their parents or a relative who they could rely on for help. "Why should anybody stick their neck out for me? Everybody's got their own things to worry about. Why should they want my problems, too?" questioned one of the girls in the study. "I called the cops once and they came and cooled my dad down, but that was it. They didn't stop him from beatin' up on us again. And my mom didn't want him arrested 'cause she was scared o' what he might do later after the cops left," remarked another girl.

The majority of children had great reservations about talking to teachers or school counselors; however, 30% indicated that they might consider asking for help if things worsened and they needed to leave the home. "I might talk to the guidance counselor if things get really bad. It's possible. I don't know for sure. Maybe," said yet another girl.

The lack of trust in the parents seemed to emanate from uncertainties about survival and lifestyle. The majority of the children exhibited doubts about their parents' ability to provide them with physical and emotional nurturance, as well as a "normal" homelife in which there were supposed to be no conflicts, with everyone living peacefully and harmoniously. They assumed that their lifestyle of constant moving and agitation was divergent from the American mainstream — that it was different and that they were,

therefore, different from most American children. On the
whole they were guarded in their optimism and were very
reluctant to predict what part, if any, their parents would
play in correcting the problem in the future.

J. Unresolved Conflicts and Ambivalence about Their Parents

Feelings of ambivalence are derived from unresolved
conflicts. There was a cause and effect relationship between
the two issues. Issues of trust, of parental role reversal, of
dependency, of love/hate, played a significantly powerful
role in undermining the resolution of conflicts between the
parents and the children. The children as a group experienced two or more of the above issues with varying degrees
of intensity and frequency. Most of the children (well over
90%) felt both love and hate for their parents, more than any
of the other ambivalences. While they expressed doubts
about their parents' love for them, they said that they loved
their parents and felt sorry for them, and at the same time
despised them. They tended to blame their parents
(particularly the abusive parent) for creating the problems
while they assumed responsibility for starting the conflicts
between their parents.

During the normal course of growing up, adolescents in
the general population are known to widen the horizons of
their relationship with their parents by increasing avenues of
communication and by participating in more cooperative
decision-making. The unilateral authority of the parent,
which characterizes most parent-child relationships before
adolescence, begins to change in the direction of mutual-
ity.[63] Parents begin by loosening the reins, so to speak, and
by encouraging participatory decision-making through
negotiation and compromise. This is not to say that most
parents abandon the controls entirely or that they are adept
in establishing truly egalitarian and democratic decision-
making processes in their families. Far from it. But these are

usually the beginning steps toward their children's eventual independence.

Parents are more likely to be specific about the control they apply over their adolescent sons and daughters. Before, it was more diffuse, more generalized. During adolescence parents tend to be more authoritarian regarding academic performance, curfews, borrowing the car, smoking. However, when confronted with problems of a personal nature, parents are generally more flexible in discussing the problem with their children and more willing to encourage reciprocity.

The adolescent children in the study do not feel that their parents are willing to loosen the reins of control or establish mutual decision-making. They characterize their parents as extremely rigid, unreasonable, very physical and emotional, out of control, poor listeners, autocratic and disinterested in how they felt or what they thought about anything. The consensus was that the parents were so caught up in their own conflicts, they could not be relied on to settle the additional conflicts that ensued between parent and child.

Everything always seemed to be approached in blacks and whites. This was a symptom of their rigidity. For this reason the term *Black and White Conflict Management*[64] was adopted to describe the process of interpersonal problem-solving that was commonly employed by most of the parents of the children in the study. This expression was coined by Roy in an attempt to explain how the parents approached conflict resolution. Most parents in the general population respond to the inevitable conflict between them and their children by being lenient or strict. Usually they are either authoritarian or permissive.[65] Commitment to either method does not necessarily lead to mutually acceptable results. The processes may even have the secondary effect of causing additional conflict.

While this is true for the general population of parents in the United States, it is also true for the parents of children who are exposed to concurrent child/wife abuse only more so. The parents who are wife-beaters or battered wives usually have a more extreme response to disagreements between them and their children. Usually the batterer becomes combative while the battered wife becomes indifferent. This extreme disparity in problem-solving approaches wreaks havoc with the children who are trying to decode the messages that their parents are transmitting to them.

The batterer employs violence as his principal method of conflict resolution. The battered wife, particularly if she is severely and chronically battered, disengages herself from the role of disciplinarian. She relinquishes her partnership in the disciplining process, hence the term *Black and White Conflict Mangement.* The key components of the method are *violence versus apathy.*

The *Black and White Conflict Management System* does not have a wide range of techniques for problem resolution. The range is narrowly confined and does not incorporate negotiation or compromise which are essential to a more effective management system. The *Black and White System* is an either/or system of extremes. The child is subjected to physical threats and violence on the one hand and ultra-leniency on the other.

Usually if parents in general tend towards authoritarian or permissive, they do so as a team. In other words, when both parents are either consistently authoritarian or consistently lenient, the children are left with the impression that they are dealing with a single style of conflict resolution and can either accept or acquiesce to it or they can rebel against it. While either style is not perfect and undesirable in the light of recent research and literature about parenting, it does not cause the complex ambivalence in the children that the *Black and White System* does.

Children who are exposed to the *Black and White System* are caught in the middle of a tug of war, not really being sure which way to turn. Their fathers lack the skills of compromise and concession. Violence in their eyes seems to be the most expedient problem-solving technique. These men are ignorant of the other various alternatives to violence. They are comfortable with violence and so do not usually on their own initiative seek to explore new methods or change the system. They have a narrow spectrum of alternatives, which do not usually broaden spontaneously. There are no tints and shades (other alternatives to violence) in the spectrum.

Their wives at the other extreme also lack skills of negotiation and compromise. While they do not usually employ physical force (this tends to occur more often *after* they leave the battering husband), their universe of tints and shades hardly exists. Most often they are overly burdened by the stressors of their relationship with their husband and cannot cope with the conflicts and disagreements they may have with the children. And so they abdicate.

The children are caught in the middle of all this turmoil. It's either "fist" or famine. Children in these situations do not develop a rich vocabulary for settling disputes. They are deprived from learning and employing a language with a high feeling content and which is issue oriented.

Because they do not learn how to verbally express their feelings and identify the issues of controversy, they are, in the opinion of this study's investigator, *ambivalence prone.* This proclivity towards ambivalence tends to be a general-ized phenomenon, having a far-reaching effect on their ability to settle disputes outside the family parameters. This accounts for the violent aggression that we see in the male adolescents who are acting out in school or who are both verbally and physically abusive with their girlfriends, and for their radical inclination (reaction) to the physcial abuse in the home by contemplating parricide in the event that circumstances become *totally intolerable.* It also accounts for the extreme behavior of the females who use the black and white solution of suicide or who run away or expose themselves to the dangers inherent in prostitution.

Because their vocabulary is limited to the language of combat — since it is a language of bodily physical aggression — to the exclusion of verbal argumentation, the children (both male and female) do not learn how to identify their feelings or to express them in positive non-threatening and non-accusatory ways. Likewise, they do not become adept at identifying the issues of conflict and are not cognitive of what they are feeling or why they are feeling it.

This ambivalence becomes apparent when the children indicate that they think that they love their parents, while at the same time they feel hatred for them. They say that they depend on them to take care of their physical needs (room and board) and that this makes them feel "bad" about hating them. The older boys resent having to protect their mothers. Many of them wish that their mothers would do something to stop the violence or that their mothers deserve the physical abuse or that their mother's behavior in some way may be responsible for the physical abuse. At the same time they feel sorry for their mothers. The girls resent not being able to bring their friends home and also dislike having to do extra chores around the house when their mother is incapacitated. They, too, feel "sorry" for their mothers and dislike them at the same time for being "weak".

These mixed emotions keep the children in a state of anxiety about how to resolve the conflicts between themselves and their parents. It's like being on a teeter-totter. They are always at the extremes of their emotions. They hate or they love (mostly feel sorry). They can't seem to balance the teeter-totter. It goes up or down. Both sides cannot remain in mid-air at once. There are no alternatives on the teeter-totter besides going up and down. This symbolizes the limited options available to the children who are confined to the teeter-totter. There is no reason to believe that the children on the teeter-totter will be able to make it do anything but go up or down unless they get off it and begin the process of exploring other options and alternatives.

Over 90% of the children indicated that they felt responsible in some way for some of the arguments between their parents. They admitted that they were not always at fault. However, because they felt guilty about, in their opinion, starting the fights some of the times, they were concerned that their behavior might cause future confrontations between the parents and lead to the physical abuse of the mother. These mixed feelings contributed to their ambivalence about the conflicts between their parents and their role as provocators.

In summary, the majority of the children in the study

lacked the skills necessary to identify their feelings, to express them in non-aggressive ways, and to pinpoint the issues of controversy between them and their parents. They were totally reliant on the *Black and White System of Conflict Management* which restricted them to a narrow band of options and alternatives. This resulted in chronic mixed feelings about their parents, thereby causing the children to be *ambivalence prone.* Unless the children were given the tools of negotiation and compromise and the experience of sorting out and exploring and identifying their feelings, there is no reason to believe that they would spontaneously generate a more positive effective communication system between themselves and their parents.

The children in describing their feelings about their parents did not differentiate between the parents' actions and the parents as persons. They did not separate the deed from the doer. Such comments as, "I can't stand my father. He's a nasty person" or "I don't really like my mom either, she's always smashed," serve as examples. Statements like these indicate that the children did not learn how to "feel" non-violently, ie., without attacking the self-esteem of another person.[66] They were not able to say, for instance, "My father's behavior makes me very angry and sad, but I still love him as a person" or "Mom's drinking makes me feel frustrated and angry, but she's a good person and I love her anyway." They were conditioned by their parents to express anger via character assassination. This includes, name-calling, swearing, cursing and employing negative unencouraging criticisms, such as, "He's such a mean person. He'll never be able to change," or "He was born with a bad temper. Mom says I'm just like him, and I'll never amount to nothin'," or "He's no good."

By not distinguishing between feelings about the inappropriate and intolerable actions of their abusive parent and the person per se, the children experienced muddled feelings and were more apt to direct their feelings against their parent's character than against their parent's negative behavior.

This, too, accounts for their ambivalence about being

loved by their parents. All of the children indicated that they were unsure or doubted their fathers loved them. Eighty percent said that they felt their mothers loved them, but there were times when they doubted it. These occurred when their mothers got angry, lost their temper and used profanities or called them degrading names.

All in all, the majority of the children did not possess the necessary skills that would enable them to communicate their feelings in non-violent and non-judgmental ways. They were "handicapped" in this area because their parents did not possess these skills and were obviously hampered in teaching them to their children. One can say with a strong degree of certainty that most parents in the general population have difficulty with expressing their feelings.

Most parents "attack" the child while disciplining them, without affirming their love for the child, and most parents punish their disobedient child without understanding that punishment stifles communication. Expressing real emotions however, such as anger at a particular behavior in conjunction with expression of love, encourage communication between parent and child. While this would tend to create ambivalences for most children, it would not necessarily limit the children to the extremes of the *Black and White System of Conflict Management*. It's a question of degree. They would be less likely to resort to physically violent solutions to their conflicts than the children whose parents relied on violence as a problem solver.

K. Transition Induced Stress

This term describes the stress that accompanies the frequent mobility of the women and children in the population. Stress occurs when external demands, such as an irate parent or internal thoughts like "What's going to happen if Mom and Dad keep fighting?" cause the person to adapt. All of us experience stress in our lives at one time or another (Charlesworth and Nathan, 1984).[67] There are differences in the kinds of stressors that affect us, as well as differences in the way we either adapt or maladapt to them. Certainly the children in the study were subjected to various kinds of internal and external stressors. However, this study did not explore the wide variety of demands on the children such as emotional, social, chemical, school, physical, disease, fear, pain or environmental stressors. This would require a full-scale study in itself.

This study did not attempt to measure the degree of stress or to determine the possible physical disorders, such as cardiovascular disease, coronary heart disease, high blood pressure, chronic headaches, etc., that very often result from too much sustained exposure to stressors. Instead it tried to determine whether or not there was a possibility that change could be a source of external stress for children in violent homes. The children were simply asked to reveal the frequency with which they either moved from their homes or ran away from home within the period of a year. At the time of the study the children were residing either in shelters for battered women, in homes for children or at the homes of friends or relatives.

Two-thirds of the population indicated that they moved from their homes about twice a year. They were usually accompanied by their mothers. More than half of the population (those in shelters for battered women) stated that this was the first time in such a refuge, and three-quarters of the children over the age of fifteen indicated that they ran away from home about twice a year. Over 85% of the population stayed with friends and relatives about twice a year. Those who were at a shelter had also stayed with friends or relatives during the course of a year. These figures were for the period of the year immediately preceding the interview and did not in any way reflect previous years' mobility patterns. In a few extreme cases some of the families used the family car as a "home" when the mothers didn't know where to turn to for shelter.

It is impossible to comment on the extent to which change as a stressor has affected the children in the study. One can say that the change of uprooting is a stressor for most people, in general, under the most favorable of conditions. People usually have to adjust to the new surroundings and new people. Having left their networks and support systems behind them, both children and adults who move from one residence to another, from one locality to another, from one city or state to another or from one country to another will undoubtedly experience the stress of change.

Therefore, children from violent homes who change their location more than twice a year most assuredly will have to cope up with the additional stress of transition. The nature of the transition will also be a source of added or heightened stress for them. Their transition to safer ground is characterized by unpredictability and fear of detection which, of course, would contribute more stress. The children usually leave during the course of a violent confrontation or immediately afterward. They may leave upon the recommendation of police officers who have responded to a dispute call to their homes or they may leave several days or weeks after a violent confrontation (the departure may have been carefully planned by the mother who has chosen to deliberately keep her plans secret until the last moment). Sometimes if there are threats against a relative (such as a mother- or father-in-law), the mother and children will leave the house and drive around aimlessly until they can get situated at a neighbor's, leave town, find public shelter, go to a church or the police. So the reality of not knowing when they will have to pick up, perhaps with nothing but the clothes on their backs, must be a gnawing stressor, to say the least.

While away from home, the children are forced to cope with new surroundings. If they leave during the week, they will miss school. If they find shelter nearby and can attend school, their books and personal belongings will not be available to them. Having to explain why they don't have required books and why they keep wearing the same clothes may be added stressors. In addition, their mother may have left without money or credit cards. Lack of money for food (lunches), snacks, gas for the car, transportation will be the source of more stress.

If the children find refuge with their mothers in shelters for battered women, they will have to put up with the specific stress that accompanies group living situations. They will have house rules, strange adults, other children. Their chaotic home lives have ill equipped them to trust adults, to negotiate and compromise, to express their feelings in non-violent ways. At most refuges they will be required to conform to a style of living that is quite unfamiliar to them. Until they can warm up to the new surroundings, there will be a period of transition that will require adaptation on several levels. In addition, it's possible that they may feel guilty about having left their father behind, and they may be less worried about practical problems such as retrieving possessions, for example, clothing, money, record collections, skateboards, stereo, makeup, etc., but they will nevertheless be upset by their loss. They may be afraid that their father might find them and carry out a previous threat, and they may harbor a more generalized fear about the unknown; what lies ahead for them in the immediate future? Will they be reunited with their father? If so, will he abuse them and their mother again? Will they find a new home? What will happen to their personal possessions? Will they ever see their friends again? Will their mother be able to provide for them?

If the children are separated from their parents and placed temporarily in a shelter, foster home, or institution because their well-being is threatened or endangered, they will experience the exacerbated stress of separation in addition to all of the other fears and concerns. A common concern for such children who lack any parental support is whether or not their placement will be long-term. Their greatest fear is that they will not be returned to their homes and that their removal from the home will be permanent. Many of these children are known to run away from such institutions, rather than be forced to have to deal will strange adults and a completely new peer group.

There are many stress factors that are associated with children from violent homes who are in transition. These pressures are associated with constant shifting from the permanent domicile. Adjustment and adaptation to new surroundings, new people, new circumstances, and new fears are required in order for the children to be able to function without noticeable impairment. However, the unpredictability of the relocation, the frequency, and the fears of detection and concerns about their immediate fate create enormous psychological pressures over the period of transition.

L. Frequent "Accidental Victims of Assault"

All of the males 15 years and older attempted to protect their mothers from being beaten by intervening during the assaults at least one time. It was during these episodes that 62% of these children were physically abused while rescuing their mothers. But abuse of these children was not confined to the sparse periods when they attempted to confront their fathers during a fight. These children, as well as the other children in the study, were also indirect victims of abuse on occasion. This usually occurred without warning when the children happened to be in the general vicinity of the argument. The father after reaching the peak of his violent episode would start throwing furniture and household objects. If the children happened to be in his path of destruction, it was possible for them to become flying objects as well. The younger the children, the more likely injuries would be serious, such as broken shoulders, ribs, concussions. Very often children who witness violence between their parents learn to physically remove themselves from the combat zone if they have the opportunity. They will run into bathrooms or bedrooms and may even run outside the house. As they get older and feel that they can successfully challenge their fathers, they are more likely to intervene in the altercation.

In more acute cases, where there is a possibility of homicide to the mother, the panic-stricken mother runs out of the house in an attempt to save her own life. Some of these cases end in devastating tragedy for the children as they will become the direct targets of the father's wrath in the absence of their mother. This could lead to the eventual death of the children. It is not unheard of for some of these children to be thrown from high-rise apartments, or shot, or beaten and stabbed to death. This may occur as a passionate response to the wife's departure or it may result after a hostage situation in which the husband barricades himself in the home and threatens to kill the children and himself. These cases are directly tied to the domestic dispute between the husband and the wife and are not commonly associated with a direct confrontation between the abusive parent and the battered children.

There is a very important lesson to be learned from the deaths of such children. Because these children may not be the primary victims of physical abuse, there is a tendency to downplay the danger that they are being exposed to as secondary victims. Because they are "accidental" victims does not in any way diminish the risks to life and well-being that they are forced to face by living in a household where the level of violence against the mother is high. Death is death and it is final. Whether the children die because they are prime targets or because they are witnesses or innocent bystanders does not make their death any less final or tragic.

The possibility of such a violent conclusion to years of violence between parents should be an issue of high priority for state authorities as they administer to the state department of social services and the state child protection coordinating committees whereby primary, secondary and tertiary prevention plans are developed and coordinated. Where there is domestic violence, there is child abuse. At times this abuse may lead, either as a result of primary vicitimization or secondary "accidental" victimization to serious injury and death to the children. In addition, resource enhancement, such as public and professional education programs, divisional, regional and local staff training and research and demonstration projects, should include this high risk population of children. Domestic violence should be considered a high risk situation for children living in these homes.

Private agencies involved in the prevention of child abuse and neglect must also spearhead a movement to include this population as fulfilling the criteria for families at risk because of the high potential for severe child abuse and neglect. Even though, heretofore, marital discord has been considered a risk factor for abuse, it has not been given priority as a major cause of child abuse and neglect. It is usually equally weighed with other stress factors, such as unemployment, family illness or unwanted pregnancy. Immediate and ongoing assistance must be offered to these families-at-risk. The identification process is extremely critical. More importantly in terms of long-term prevention, the earlier the identification and the earlier the intervention, the greater the effect on the incidence of abuse.

Shelters for battered women have a particularly critical role to play in establishing networks of services with local and state authorities. They will be an important source of information and can serve as training banks for social service personnel. Shelter staff can act as change agents by helping to design and construct training packages for in-service training programs in their communities and by working with the police and especially with hospital administrators in developing similar strategies, protocol and programs for their appropriate personnel. Shelters can also be parenting oases for the mothers, and in some instances where they offer counselling services for batterers, for fathers by connecting them with parent effectiveness training programs in their communities and in the communities where the mothers and children may eventually relocate. It is helpful for shelters to offer on-site positive parenting programs including training that will increase the parents' competency skills in the area of physical care and supervision. By relying on shelters for battered women as primary resources for referrals and expertise, communities will benefit enormously in the long run. The majority of the sheltering programs in localities across the nation do not offer long-term shelter for battered women and their children. This is usually because they have limited space and limited financial resources for this purpose. More to the point, it is because there is a half-hearted commitment from local and state authorities and from other public and private sources of revenue. Historically shelters for battered women and children have not been given the unanimous support of communities that the children's sheltering and child welfare movement has been given. There has been subtle and tacit opposition to the sheltering movement for battered women and children. This has hampered their growth and prolifer-ation. In some quarters, they are considered controversial because they are mistakenly viewed as radical political extensions of a feminist plot to break up families. As a result most shelters are forced to take on a low profile in their communities. Low profile dooms these shelters to low priority and a low notch on the totem pole of social issues.

Despite the fact that a recent national study[68] indicates that the incidence of wife-beating is down over the past decade, official reports (documented cases taking refuge in the 700 plus refuges around the country) show that shelters are still bursting at the seams and that the demand for protective services is still as great, if not more, than it was ten years ago.

To my knowledge there are no shelters for battered women which do not also permit their children to reside with them. The refuge movement since its inception in 1975 has always included the co-sheltering and protection of children. By offering sanctuary to wives whose lives are endangered, they are simultaneously offering protective services to the children who accompany them. On the average each battered woman usually brings two children with her. In reality, shelters for battered women are havens for children as well and are performing a protective function that should be the responsibility of local, state and federal authorities. These centers are brimming with children of all ages. Although they are providing a lifesaving function for the children in them, they are rarely totally or in large part funded by government support. This may have the positive effect of political and structural autonomy which may be preferred by many shelter programs. However, it does not give the community the benefit of choice and flexibility in designing programs which could possibly be wider in scope. There is always more to be gained from having more sources of financial support than from having fewer.

M. Confused Values

Values are part of a system that provides a framework for unconscious beliefs about the individual and the world in which he lives. Values are imparted both by individuals who are in constant and close proximity, such as parents, as well as by individuals such as teachers and religious leaders who are not quite so intimate but because of their stature in the community exert an enormous influence over our lives. Values in today's complex and fast-paced world are also transmitted via electronic media, which bombard the individual with standards that may or may not contradict one's beliefs.

The adolescent usually finds himself in a quandary when he tries to sort out which values are important, which should be challenged and which should be abandoned. Adolescence is a period of great emotional and physical upheaval. It is a time for growth but it is also a time of universal confusion. It's a period when young people begin to question the mores and beliefs that have been ingrained in them during the course of their childhood. The system under scrutiny acts as a catalyst for healthy rebellion and usually the individual, through the process of rejection and acceptance, comes to terms with what is meaningful in his life. This period of questioning and evaluation is important in the eventual emergence of the young person as a responsible contributing member of society.

It is important that the adolescent be given reasonable freedom to explore the values of the establishment. He should be encouraged to do so. He should feel unthreatened and unthwarted in his quest for understanding the systems that infiltrate his everyday world. Parents have the responsibility to instill wholesome and sound values from which adolescents can judge what they see and hear.

Adolescents cannot be expected to judge and think the way adults do. They need guidance from parents who most often have more knowledge, background and experience upon which to base judgments.

What then do young people with violent parents learn about the world around them? First and foremost, they learn that might is right. They learn that the bigger and stronger one is, the more control one can exert over another person. One learns from this the value of physical domination.

Second, the adolescent learns that there is a hierachy to the system, a real pecking order. The younger and weaker one is the more vulnerable. One learns that children cannot win in such a system. It is a no-win situation. They learn to capitulate to the system and very often react to it in maladaptive ways. They also learn from this that when they grow up (particularly relevant to the boys), they will be permitted to employ physical force in order to get results. They learn to respect violence and to employ it whenever their own situation gives them the upper hand on the hierarchy. This could happen in altercations between siblings, with pets and with peers.

Outside the insular value system of one's immediate environment there is another message. Husbands and wives are supposed to "love" one another. So how is it that my dad beats my mom if he's supposed to love her? The children in the study did not have an answer to the question. Most of them said that they didn't know if he loved her or if he didn't.

What else do they learn? They come to believe that men are stronger than women and that women and children make perfect victims of physical abuse because they can be victimized behind the closed portals of the home. They begin to notice that it is easy to get away with violence against women and children. They learn fast that the neighbors aren't going to get involved or that the local police aren't going to cart the abuser off to jail as a rule.

Another message has to do with controlling emotions. The traditional male is characterized as a cool emotionless entity. To express one's feelings is tantamount to being a wimp or a weakling.

There is fierce competition in the world and success requires that the male become a cool calculating competitor. Yet there is a contradiction. It's okay to express anger and all the other emotions in the spectrum of feelings must then dissolve into anger. In extreme situations anger leads to rage, which leads to physical violence. The end result is that sadness, fear, depression, disappointment, frustration, unhappiness, etc., get simplified into one emotion: anger. The male learns less and less how to experience the full timbre of his emotional potential.

What one learns from this is that in order to compete in this world, one must abandon the expression of emotion with one exception, anger. The more emotionally bankrupt one is, the more masculine one is apt to become. The children in the study revealed that they thought it was more important to hide one's emotions than it was to ventilate them. Real men were big and mean and desirable women were petite and cowering.

For the most part, the population reflected the typical values and confusions of our society — the values of a competitive society. On the one hand, society holds competition in high esteem, but it also strives for equality. It praises individuality but on the other hand it also suggests that we be cooperative and work together to achieve our goals. To add even more confusion to the topic, cooperation and compromise are regarded as anti-masculine. So many different messages are pushed out at us. It is no wonder that young people growing up today are bewildered.

How often are our children told that competition can be constructive — that it is associated with assertiveness and that it can build character and stir the mind and heart to achieve greatness. Winning at all costs is another typical value of our society. Children are encouraged to win the soccer game, win the 100-meter-dash, win the spelling bee, win this and win that. If winning is so revered, how then do we as a society live with losing?

It is impossible to be a winner without a loser and yet we are all striving to beat the other person over the head before our heads are chopped off. This value system is one that encourages the dehumanization of our fellow man. It is a system taken to the extreme will allow for the victimization of women and children because they are biologically smaller and less physically strong. They can be overpowered by brute force. And isn't this just another version of winning by intimidation?

N. Evidence of Perpetuation of Cycle in Teen Couples

There was mounting evidence that the young boys and girls who participated in the study were on their way to becoming the next generation of wife-beaters and battered women. Eighty-three percent of the males who were dating revealed that they hit their girlfriend(s) when they got angry at her/them. They tended to minimize the behavior by describing the situations as "nothing serious".

"She made me so mad because she was late for the dance, that I thought she shouldn't do that to me again," said one boy while describing how he managed to pull his girlfriends hair and twist her arm. Most of the descriptions usually emphasized a justification for the battering behavior. The girlfriend was most always perceived as a provocateur causing them to get angry and respond with a physical reprimand. Another boy said that he pushed his girlfriend down a flight of stairs in the Junior High School they both attended because he thought that she was lying to him.

Fifty-two percent of the girls in the study who had boyfriends said that they had arguments with them and at times they push and shove each other, scream at their boyfriends and use profanities. They, too, did not seem to be overly concerned about where these behaviors might lead. It was quite obvious that unless these children were discouraged from continuing to behave towards each other in this manner, they were going to repeat the assaultive patterns they witnessed at home. The children did not feel that they needed counselling services or intervention of any kind. They felt that they could control their own behavior and that they were not going to trust an adult to change them.

O. Cynicism about Their Own Future

The basis for the cynicism noted in the population was, no doubt, the lack of trust in adults. The children expressed clear uncertainties about the sincerity and motives of adults. They were not goal oriented. Ninety-one percent of the children said that they weren't sure what was happening to them and that they were not aware of any long-range plans either. Common responses to, "What do you think your life will be like a year from now?" were, "Probably not good" or "More of the same" or "I'm afraid to think about what it might be" or "I don't really care" or "I don't know; it's hard to say" or "It could be better, but who knows? It could be a lot worse" or "What difference does it make? It can't get too much better."

Their fears, self-doubts, stress, drug use and maladaptive coping mechanisms overloaded the circuits to developing a more hopeful picture of what lay ahead in their immediate future. Speculation about the future was not something that seemed entirely relevant to them. They were more concerned about survival on a day-to-day basis. They learned from their experiences living with violence in the home that one minute things could be fine and peaceful, then in an instant the situation could change radically. By the time they were adolescents they learned that it would serve no purpose to hope for a better future or to trust that things would dramatically improve. They were seasoned cynics. Their attitude was the culmination of a childhood that reinforced feelings of doubt, despair, sorrow, fear, abandonment, frustration, anger and insecurity. It was for them an attitude that was the consequence of living in a home where physical violence dominated the normal course of events.

Discussion

The sample of American children between the ages of 11 and 17 provided insights into the effects that marital violence has had upon them. The study is valuable because of its use of children as a primary source of information. The mixed group of boys and girls in the study were chosen as subjects because they met two major criteria:

1. They were articulate and positively disposed towards discussing their experiences.
2. Wife-beating was a serious problem in their family background.

Most of the key areas of discussion did not present any discernible concern or discomfort in the children. However, many of the children expressed uneasiness about probing responses to questions about their fear of themselves (referred to above as auto-phobia). The inevitable conclusion (parricide and/or homicide) to the steady and consistent years of childhood exposure to violence between their parents was ladened with fears that without intervention such conclusions might be realized. This thought was profoundly burdensome.

Not all of the children in the study were affected in the same way or in the same degree. The effects varied. In addition, about 90% of the children experienced all of the problems alluded to in the study. It was extremely important to gain the trust and confidence of this cynically inclined population. Establishing rapport from the first encounter and presentation of the project description is crucial in developing a sizable and reliable sample. The population is at best a difficult one to probe. So it was critical to determine from the outset what course of presentation and format would be most likely to be accepted by the youngsters.

Feelings and perceptions are guarded in our society; expressing them might render a person vulnerable. How to establish rapport, create a non-threatening dynamic environment and sustain the cooperation of a group of challenging youngsters was a problem that had to be surmounted if the study was to occur at all. The decision was, therefore, made for the examiner to be as open and as straightforward about the study as possible, emphasizing the importance and value of the study for other children in similar circumstances. It was also important for them to know that the interviewer was a person with credibility in the field and that there was a genuine interest in these children as people. In other words, the study was important, but only secondary to the impor-tance of the children participating in it. It was essential to inform the children that they were not compelled to answer all of the questions, and that they could drop out of the study at any time if they so desired.

The initial presentations were made in a group setting. This proved to be advantageous. The youngsters enjoyed the attention they were getting from the investigator and seemed eager to exchange their intimate encounters with everyone. The girls were interviewed separately as were the boys. The girls seemed to enjoy the group process more than the boys. But eventually both groups warmed up to the discussions.

In order for the children to believe that they had a personal stake in the study, they had to feel that this study was their study. In order to accomplish this goal the investigator abandoned the idea of asking a set of precon-ceived questions. The children had to feel that they owned the study. The best way to achieve this purpose was to ask the children to develop the instrumentation, ie., to help create the issues that were important to them, that they thought would have application for others in their age group and that would be helpful to adults working with the population. It was helpful to say to them that this was an opportunity for them to help others and also to get some things off their chests. This approach proved enormously successful. Naturally, the study took longer. But the personal touch, the sincerity of intention and the importance of their input in creating the instrumentation was largely responsi-ble for the cooperation and enthusiasm of the participants.

How to address the children was a pressing question. Were they to be referred to as kids, children, young adults, young people? None of the above? The term *other people your age* went unchallenged. But more importantly, it was critical to learn the name of everyone in the group as quickly as possible and to employ names as frequently as possible during the course of the study. Having developed the instrumentation through group process, the transition to individual one-on-one, in-depth interviews went smoothly. The process took hours and weeks to complete but it was worthwhile in the end because it cut down on the possible number of withdrawals from this study and it created a positive environment for understanding some of the intimate devastating effects of marital violence on the children.

Conclusions

The following conclusions were drawn from the study:

1. Violence between husbands and wives causes a great deal of physical pain and psychological anguish in their children.
2. Forty percent of the children were regularly physically abused by either parent, the father being the primary abuser.
3. When the women and the children left the abusive home, the mother in 85% of the cases became the primary abuser.
4. Twenty-eight percent of the females reported sexual abuse, 10% of which had been documented with child protective services.
5. Forty-one percent of the fathers were reported to have a drinking problem; eight percent smoked pot and two percent were purported to take more potent drugs.
6. Twenty-four percent of the mothers were reported to have a drinking problem to "forget the beatings".
7. All males 15 years of age and older tried ro rescue their mother during a violent argument at least one time. About 10% of the total population intervened on one occasion.
8. Sixty percent of the boys were in trouble with school authorities at one time or another for truancy and fist fights.

9. Eighty-five percent of the children admitted to a drinking problem which started as early as age eleven; two percent started at age nine.

10. Ten percent of the population suffered from chronic enuresis and insomnia.

11. Truancy, running away, drug and alcohol abuse, drug dealing, prostitution, assaultive behavior were common coping techniques.

Individual Portraits

Painting Pictures with Tarnished Remembrances and Fractured Dreams

Sacred family! . . . The supposed home of all the virtues, where innocent children are tortured into their first falsehoods, where wills are broken by parental tyranny, and self-respect smothered by crowded, jostling egos.

(August Strindberg, *The Son of a Servant*, 1886)

CHAPTER 5

King of the House: My Dad Was More than Just a Father

"My mom knew what was going on between my father and me and my older sister. Every time she tried to stop him from bothering us, my dad would hit her or choke her. He's almost killed her a couple of times. She'd get it anytime she would try to interfere. He thinks of himself as king of the house; whenever things don't go his way, he's bound to punch out my mom and then when he calms down, he's all over my sister or me," confided Jessie a pleasant-looking sixteen-year-old whose seemingly affable outward appearance belied the gruesome tragedy of her real life experience.

I listened with heightened sensitivity as I tried to keep my professional composure and thus continue the interview. Jessie was deeply troubled and scarred with haunting memories of her recent past. Her family history was marred by the raging tyrant, her father. He was a thorn in her side, but she was determined, as contradictory as it may have sounded, to write a happy ending to the script of her personal tragic drama. She harbored dreams, perhaps fantasies of days to come when she and her mom and dad and her three older brothers and her older sister would be reunited and live happily ever after. She wanted this more than anything. I could almost taste her wish-dream. She wanted it badly. Her desire was so utterly visceral that I sat in my straight-back wooden chair and gripped the highly polished wood table that separated Jessie from me.

It was painful to sit opposite this tortured, yet poised, young female. She had grown up so fast, long before most girls her age. She had been denied the normal playful years of childhood. Instead Jessie's world was burdened with a childhood better forgotten than remembered, and yet I could not help but sense the utter relief she felt by baring all during that intimate series of meetings we had the winter of 1982-83. She willingly volunteered to talk with me about her experiences at home. More accurately, she looked forward to our weekly rendezvous.

Jessie was soft spoken but assertive. She could have conveniently hedged some of the more jolting questions about her relationship with her father, but she chose to respond straightforwardly and in unhaltingly good humor.

The interviews were a beginning. Jessie could unburden herself without fear of judgment or reprisals. She had already taken the most important step in her life when she confided in a guidance counselor during her sophomore year in high school. This was a monumental decision for her. It meant betraying her own flesh and blood. More importantly, it signified her deep interest in reversing a process of self-loathing and agony that would someday help to initiate the massive healing that needed to take place in the spirit of her personhood.

She began by describing her mother, a woman driven to the artificial utopia of a feelingless world by an eleven-year-old addiction to Valium. "There is a doctor where we live who keeps her supplied with all the Valium she needs," said Jessie. "Mom is a petite women who is very nervous. If she doesn't have her pills, she gets cranky and yells at everybody and gets in a crazy mood. She doesn't know what's happening. Whenever I went home for a visit, she looked spaced out. My dad would try to stop her from taking the pills by taking them away from her, but she would go get more."

I got the impression from what Jessie said that her mother's maladaptive coping method of escaping the trials and tribulations of daily life made sense to her. Jessie understood her mother's escape from reality. How else could this woman put up with so much abuse for so many years? Jessie's voice cracked in one rare moment of vulnerability when she talked about her mother's mental and physical condition. She had always remembered her mother this way.

Her mother started using Valium when Jessie was five years old. The woman who had given birth to her was in Jessie's world of memories a living ghost who had created for herself an invisible drug-infested protective shield to render her impervious to the harsh blows and barbs of her pugnacious husband. Her mother was a phantom, a sad reminder of a lonely loveless childhood. Jessie seemed to echo this ghostlike quality of half living in this world. Although she herself was not addicted to Valium, she appeared passionless about her plight. After all, her role model for all her 16 years was this fragile broken-down woman who she referred to as her mom.

An older sister, who had failed to extricate herself from the brutal and lecherous clutches of her father, remained at home, a continuing victim of his battery and incest. She is 11 years older than Jessie and lives at home with her mother and father and three younger brothers, ranging in age from 21 to 26. Her life was further complicated by the birth of a baby girl when she was about 25 years of age. There is a strong possibility that the child was sired by her father, although she had a boyfriend at the time. Her sister never resolved the matter. She refused a blood test for fear that her father would retaliate if she publicized the possibility.

Jessie does not feel that there is much hope for her sister. She feels that she has been under her father's clutches for too long. The only liberation for her would be in her father's

voluntary exile from the home or after his death. She thinks
that her sister will never take the initiative to leave home
and try to make it on her own. Her life has been so wretched
that she will need extraordinary assistance from the outside
world if she is to survive on her own and Jessie feels that this
is not forthcoming.

"Dad is six foot one and in his fifties. He's really fat, about
245 pounds and balding. His stomach protrudes due to all
the beer he drinks. His arms are very muscular. He has a
problem with beer. For example, one day he went out to a
bar at three o'clock in the afternoon and didn't come home
until 1 a.m. the next morning. He drinks like this about three
times a week. One thing, he doesn't drink at home. All of his
drinking takes place outside the home in bars. He's been a
steelworker ever since his discharge from the Navy, quitting
school after the tenth grade," revealed Jessie.

She continued, "Mom, who is only four feet eleven
inches, finished high school while Dad was in the Navy. She
was really smart. But she never worked after they got
married. She stayed at home and had one kid after another.
Her mother, my grandmother, was put into a nursing home
at age 58 and died at 71. We'd visit her every other Sunday.
They say she died of a broken heart because no one in the
family wanted to take her in after my grandfather suddenly
died of a heart attack. He was a construction worker. That's
all I really know about him."

Jessie reached back in her memories. She stated that her
paternal grandmother, who is still living at age 97, was and
still is, an unusual woman. Her life was crisscrossed by work
and pregnancy, work and pregnancy. Her grandfather, a
wife-beater and child abuser, would stay at home long
enough to impregnate his wife, and then abruptly leave until
three weeks after the delivery. His behavior was remarkably
consistent. He could be relied on to adhere to this blatantly
irresponsible pattern of wife and child neglect for all nine of
his wife's pregnancies. Jessie attributed this outrageous
conduct to his drinking problem. She said that he was
addicted to beer and, "He didn't want to think about
nothing else." He died five years before Jessie was born so

all of her information was transmitted orally to her. Her prime historical source, of course, was her grandmother.

I began to detect an element of pride in Jessie's discourse. She began to play a different melody. Her voice steadied and her pitch rose. She was obviously very proud of her paternal grandmother. Perhaps, I thought, this could be the *significant other* in Jessie's life. There was a strong possibility that her grandmother had been an enormous positive role model for her while she was growing up. Certainly her grandmother's stamina and independent spirit were to be admired. What is interesting is that she lived right next door to Jessie and her family and continued at age 97 to reside there and take care of herself, in spite of the fact that she has arthritis and can't get around much anymore. To Jessie she was as strong as the Rock of Gibraltar.

Jessie's dad was the youngest of the brood. She remembered that her father, once during a drunken episode, had stated that he wanted to be like his own father. This, she interpreted to mean, that he wanted to drink and beat up his wife and kids, just as Jessie's grandfather had done to his wife and kids. Unlike his father, he was not an absentee parent, working steadily to support the family throughout the marriage. He and her mom would get into heated fights over the childen. Jessie thought that there was more to the arguments than just trivialities.

She reflected, "I think that they really didn't want to have five kids, maybe just one. The fights were really about us kids being in their way and that if they could do it over, we'd be out of the picture." She felt that her father felt more strongly about this than her mother. Her mother spent the better part of their childhood trying to impress her husband with the kid's good grades but, "He never really had faith in us," said Jessie. "He didn't think that we were smart. He just took the good grades for granted. When it was report card time and we got good grades, he'd say that the next report wouldn't be good. All of us kids had B averages, which I think was good, but Dad didn't give us credit for it. He didn't have very high expectations for us.

"Holidays around our house were pretty nice. Dad and

Mom never fought during Christmastime. But about two or three weeks later, it would suddenly hit him that he'd spent too much money on us and all hell'd break loose. It got so that it was hard to enjoy the holiday knowing that there'd be fireworks about the gifts and money later on," said Jessie. But the typical scenario of fights and blood and gore which took place on a regular basis was vividly recollected by Jessie. She remembered things that happened when she was ten years of age. That's when he started to get very physically violent. Jessie recalled that the violence was once connected with his drinking bouts. However, he soon became violent whether he was drunk or sober. There was no telling what would trigger him off. Sometimes there didn't seem to be any reason for the violence.

"He'd come home and demand supper from my mom. Once he put her head through the mirrored medicine chest and broke the glass. Mom threw up after this, but he wouldn't let up. He screamed at her to get dinner. When she refused, he put her head through the plasterboard in the kitchen," Jessie remembered.

"When I was ten, Dad started to mess around with my sister. We shared the same bedroom so I know. He did it in front of me. He wouldn't bother me the way he did her, but he did start kissing me the way he wasn't supposed to. He said that all fathers did this. I didn't know anything," she continued. "Sis tried to get out of his clutches. One time she moved out on her own, but my father said that she was whoring around town and so he went to bring her back home and got a shotgun and he told her if she didn't come back, he'd blow off her head. She believed him. This was when she was about 22. She lived with a roommate who worked with her. The roommate and the landlord were there when Dad threatened my sister. And my dad told the landlord to get out of the way. When he didn't, my dad punched him. He got a $50 fine for that. So, my sister came back home and quit her job after about a month. She never left after this because she always feared that he would come after her. Dad never liked anybody leaving home. He'd get very angry when he couldn't dominate us."

Jessie's voice dropped. She seemed weary and deject
This was a good time in the interview to shift the emphas...
away from the human side. I was curious about what her
home and it environs were like. Jessie bounced back. She
began by describing her house as an eyesore in a very
pleasant neighborhood where most of the people took care
of their homes. While she described her home with all of its
dinginess, I couldn't help thinking about the film, *The
Picture of Dorian Gray*. This ramshackle house with missing
siding and a broken-down screen door at the front was a
tangible *object* of the decay within. Big ditches surrounded
the house, dug by her father during some long ago
"irrigation project" which he had never completed. There
was junk and metal scraps all over the place, in the front yard
and out back. It seems that Jessie's father thought he was an
inventor and that someday he would be able to use the junk
to produce a marketable invention.

"The neighbors thought that we were low class. We never
associated with them. It was just as well. Dad didn't want
anyone coming over and snooping around our place,"
stated Jessie. She continued to describe her home. She
mentioned that although there was no garage or carport, her
father insisted on having a black Cadillac which stood out in
hilarious incongruity. Jessie laughed as we talked about his
incessant obsession with black Cadillacs. The one-story
wood frame house, which was in ruins, was the backdrop for
this sparkling black Cadillac — her father's pride and joy.

This memory afforded the comic relief so sorely needed.
Jessie perked up and continued to remember the home of
her childhood. There were three bedrooms for five children
and two parents. It seemed that the two girls shared one of
the bedrooms while the other was taken up by two of the
three brothers.

They didn't have to worry about the oldest brother since
he ran away from home when he was 13 years old, got into
trouble with the law and landed in prison. Subsequently he
married and just recently got divorced. He ran away because
he and his father didn't get along. There were always fights.
He'd invariably get blamed for everything that went wrong.

Jessie recalled what her mother had said to her about the
time when her dad demolished the boy's Harley Davidson
bike with a sledge hammer. It happened when Jessie was
too young to remember. She attempted to explain why this
occurred by reasoning that her father's jealousy drove him
to it.

"He didn't want us to have nothing. I guess my dad
thought them bikes cost a lot. My brother paid for it with his
own money which he had saved from his job at the pizza
shop. He was real upset about the bike. It's what made him
run away," said Jessie.

"He hung around town for a while and then got involved
with drug dealing. He used to come home for visits. He and
my mom never got along for some reason. One time they
got into a fist fight and he blackened her eyes. Mom was so
angry that she screamed at him to leave and never come
back. She said that she was disowning him then and there.
The next time we heard about him he was in prison on a
drug bust. He spent two and a half years in jail. He was
hooked on cocaine at the time, but doesn't do drugs now.
When we saw him after his probation he told us that he got
married and had a little girl but the marriage didn't work
out. He's back home now. My mom doesn't like to talk
about it. I really don't know if they're getting along."

In addition to the three small bedrooms there was a
kitchen and a living room. The house had no bathtub,
shower or sink in the bathroom. Her family *bathed* in a small
basin in the bathroom. They didn't have hot water and so
had to boil water to wash themselves. The kitchen had the
usual amenities: refrigerator, sink and gas stove. There was
a raggedy chair in the living room and a sofa that was too old
and too dilapidated to offer support or comfort. There was,
of course, the inevitable TV. And that was it. The inside and
outside were in an advanced state of disrepair. Jessie stated
that the other homes in the area had well tended lawns and
flower gardens. They in no way seemed to resemble the
squalor she was used to.

"Mom was often abused," Jessie stated at the opening of
our next encounter. "She never told anybody about the real

reason why she had bruises over her body. She never wanted anyone to know. One winter when she had a black eye, she wore sunglasses for a week. She never talked to the neighbors. She always felt inferior and ashamed. She felt most uncomfortable about the way she looked. I mean the way she dressed. She usually wore raggedy pants and stained blouses. It was hard to get clothes really clean without hot water," continued Jessie.

She could never remember anyone coming over to visit, or her parents going out to a movie or to dinner. They always stayed at home.

Summers were spent at the house. Jessie wasn't even allowed to go down the street to play with other children in the neighborhood. She confessed that every once in a while she'd sneak away and meet at her girlfriend's house. Her parents didn't want to associate with neighbors and they never attended school functions.

Most of the two-hundred and sixty dollars a week paycheck that her father brought home went for his beer. This left no money for other essentials, such as food and clothing, let alone recreation. To complicate matters, he'd gamble whatever he could save up from his paychecks on the horses. Sometimes he'd take Jessie with him to the races and blame her if his horse would lose. Every once in a while, Jessie would get to go to the movies with her sister. But it was hard to save up for the price of an admission ticket on a dollar fifty cent a week allowance.

What Jessie wanted more than anything was to learn how to swim. However, her father denied her access to a community pool that was within walking distance. It was not a question of money. Jessie could have afforded the fifty-cent admission cost. It was more a question of keeping the family isolated from the community at large. And so Jessie could only dream about what it must have been like to spend a summer's day swimming at the nearby pool.

Visits to the doctor whenever a family member was sick were rare. Jessie confided that her parents didn't trust doctors. They looked with disdain upon the medical profession in general. They guarded the family's medical history and feared that the abuse and incest might be discovered by the doctor.

Jessie then began to reveal some of the more intimate details of the sordid relationship between her older sister and their father. It seems that her father was the catalyst for her drug addictions.

"He started her on drinking and smoking pot," said Jessie. "Then he'd drive her to a local motel every Friday night and drop her off so that she could pick up somebody and she wouldn't come home 'til the next morning. It was like he was selling her . . . ," Jessie continued. Her voice dropped.

"He even tried to get me to go out with a 35-year-old man and said he'd show me a good time and all. This guy was a married man my dad knew from work. But I didn't agree to it, no way. One time he said he'd give me $75 if I let him take nude pictures of me with his Polaroid. He said he was going to show them to his buddies at the bars. He wanted to brag about his daughter to them. I got out of that one. I told him I had a headache and went to bed. By that time he passed out from drinking. He was strange."

Jessie kept talking non-stop. She easily went from one recollection to another. She spoke about the first intimate encounters with her father. They began with passionate kissing episodes she could not understand. She doubted her father's cavalier explanation that all fathers kissed their daughters in such a way. When she went to a girlfriend for confirmation, she learned her father was atypical. She was subsequently shunned by her friend after that revelation.

Her mother knew what was happening. "One night she came into my room and told him to get out, but he didn't pay any attention to her. It got so my sister would cry whenever he'd come into the room. I was about 14 years old at the time and so he began to come after me. When I tried to fight him off he'd accuse me of being a lesbian. So I went out and got myself a boyfriend, but this infuriated him more. I think he was jealous. All I could do was cry and carry on and hope that he'd fall asleep. It was then that I decided to talk to my guidance counselor at school. My nerves were edgy and I didn't want to have to face my dad anymore," Jessie stated.

Jessie was temporarily removed from her home and placed in a foster home. However, when she failed to tell her foster parents that she was going out for a walk, they decided to give her up. She was then returned to her family and a repentant father who was kind to her and who begged forgiveness. However, he was back to his old ways within two weeks of Jessie's return.

Jessie said, "My dad was really nice to me the first two weeks I was home. I said that I forgave him. But then he started taking off my clothes and kissing me. I was kicking and screaming at him. My mom said that she was going to call the cops. That's when I ran away. Mom was picking up the phone — that was my last memory.

"I went to my best friend's home. I trusted my friend because she had gone through the same thing with her father, who is a high-ranking military officer. She and her mother were sympathetic. They said that they knew that something was wrong when they found out that I had been in a foster home. I told them them all the details that night and they called my social worker.

"I was placed in another foster home the next day, but it didn't work out either because it was a real messy place. I didn't think that there could be foster homes like that. There was filth all over the place and the man took me in his room and showed me a picture of a naked girl. He drank too and there were guns all over the place. I called my worker and asked her to take me out of the place, but she refused. She said my new family would do me a lot of good. I couldn't believe her. She didn't believe me."

The fact that Jessie's father had been responsible for creating an unfit home for his family remains an unfortunate tragedy. But how do we explain the neglectful and recklessness of a state department of social services' worker who created a double jeopardy for this minor by failing to protect her health and welfare. Is she too culpable for the events following that misguided foster home placement?

Jessie continued talking about this sexually aggressive foster parent. "He wanted to know how I'd like trading places with the nude girl in the picture. I said, 'No way.' His

wife worked; she left very early in the morning and he'd
wake me up. He'd come over to my bed and get mushy. I
don't know why," she declared, "the people who pick foster
homes didn't see that this wasn't suitable. I finally got out of
there. I ran away."

Jessie stated, "She (my social service worker) blamed me
for running away. She said that it was my fault. So she gave
me a choice of going back to the foster home or going back
to my real parents. I chose my own home. But it turned out
to be a disaster. My father was always drunk. He tried to
choke me because he wanted me to go to my room. My
mom and two of my brothers were home, but they didn't do
nothin'. My niece was screaming her head off and he said
he'd hit her if she didn't shut up, so she screamed even
louder. He let go and told me to get out of his sight. I ran to
my room and during the middle of the night I sneaked out
and went to the local fire company for help. I stayed there
for a couple of nights, but then I ran out of money.

"My worker found me on the streets and brought me back
home. I stayed there all summer and then it started all over
again. So I asked my grandmother for some help and she
gave me a couple of hundred dollars and I stayed in a hotel
for a few nights.

"Then an old boyfriend of mine who's on probation saw
me walking down the street and he hit me over the back of
my head with his helmet because he was mad at me because
a few days earlier I had taken back a bike that I had loaned
him. I was knocked out and fell down on the sidewalk. My
friend at the fire company phoned for an ambulance. My
parents were called down to the hospital and were asked to
take me home until I could be placed in a foster home. They
were told by my worker to keep me there anyway they had
to. And so they boarded up the windows. They put me in my
room and nailed a board across the door. I felt like a
prisoner. I didn't eat while I was in there.

"After a day I tried to escape by picking at the door with
a knife. My dad heard the noise and put chains on the door
so I couldn't get out. My mom and brothers took turns
guarding me. I knew that Mom wouldn't be a good

watchman because of all the drugs she was taking, and so I started a fire in my room when she was on guard duty. She opened the door when she smelled smoke and I ran out as fast as I could. As I was running down the cinder block staircase, she threw my brother's old army boot at me and knocked me down. I fell and hit my head and was dazed. I didn't know what was going on. I heard the fire trucks and ambulance and police. My dad said that I had overdosed on pills. He showed them a bottle of empty pills. The next thing I know is my stomach was being pumped for no good reason. They found nothing. I stayed in the hospital that day where arrangements were made for me to come to this group home until my worker can come up with another foster home.

"She's looking for a home with a husband and wife who are both working. My worker is in her late forties. She was never married and she tells me that I should never get married. I have a boyfriend now. She thinks he's no good and she always tells me, 'Never get married.' She comes out to see me every three to four months. There are only three workers in this town. I tried to get switched, but they all have a caseload of over 60 kids, so I'm stuck with my worker. I even tried to get emancipated by getting a job, but they don't trust me because of the times that I ran away."

The subsequent encounters between Jessie and me focused upon her feelings and her hopes and dreams. She was very perceptive. She talked freely about her first foster home placement as being a pleasant environment. There were two other children placed with the foster parents — a husband and wife in their mid-fifties. They were a very religious family, worshipping several times a week.

Jessie said, "If you did something wrong, or if you had a problem, they liked talking it out, but you know sometimes you can't talk out your problems. They were the kind of people who learn to love you right away. But, if you couldn't talk to them, they really got upset. That's why I felt I had to be alone the time that I went for a walk and didn't happen to tell them where I was going. I think that they were disappointed in me. I also think that they were probably hurt because it was so hard for me to confide in them so soon. They didn't really know all of the details about me and I feel that they didn't understand why I couldn't trust them right off the bat. They thought that I didn't appreciate what they were trying to do for me. I did, but it was hard for me to express myself to these strangers who were supposed to be my new family.

"I've written to them since I left. They even wanted me back, but my worker refused to place me back with them. I don't understand a lot of the reasons why my worker did what she did. All I know is that she made a lot of mistakes. It really bothered me. They wanted me back, but she just wouldn't agree to it."

I then asked Jessie to discuss in detail what had happened when she went on that solitary walk and she began to reveal the startling facts. I remember sitting there that morning feeling astonished by her description of the most perplexing events of an afternoon that could have been her last day on earth.

It was winter and snow was on the ground. Jessie had wandered away from her foster parents' house seemingly to visit a friend of hers who was living not far from them. She told me that while on her way, she began to play with a "lonely little dog that nobody owned." She was overcome by dizziness and passed out in the snow. It wasn't until three and a half hours later that a young man on his way through the woods had discovered her half-frozen and limp body. She was unconscious when found, so he ran down to a nearby garage where he summoned help. She was brought to the garage where a number of the men tried to get her to come round with mouth to mouth resuscitation while awaiting an ambulance which eventually rushed her to a nearby hospital. It was a pretty close call. She was in bad shape on arrival. Both her feet were bleeding; they had swelled up from the cold temperature causing the skin to crack and subsequently to bleed.

I was curious and I began to probe Jessie about her decision to walk into the woods that day. There was something missing in her account. I couldn't put my finger on it, but I just couldn't accept the fact that she had become dizzy and passed out. It had to be more complicated than that. I asked her if she had any recollection of what had happened and if she had felt scared about almost dying. She said that she couldn't remember a lot of the details, but that she felt "cozy" about being unconscious. This made me shudder. I began to think that maybe her innocent trek through the woods was not a spontaneous unplanned accident. We continued to talk about the circumstances that led up to her near-fatal walk.

And then she dropped the bomb. She did it during the course of our conversation without blinking an eye. It came out of her mouth like an item on a grocery list. There was no passion, no drama, no discomfort. I might have missed it if I had not been fine tuned into our dialogue. Jessie simply stated that right before entering the woods she had had an argument with her boyfriend. She did not elaborate on it, but merely stated this disturbing fact. And then it became clear to me that Jessie's lingering hours in the woods on that frosty winter day could have been her attempt to numb the deep pain of rejection and loneliness that were all too familiar to her. The rift between her and her boyfriend may have set off a chain reaction of profound depression and despair, feelings that could have led her to look upon the black abyss of death as comforting and "cozy". Jessie chuckled when she said the word, "cozy".

Her mood changed when she related how bothered she had been by her worker's refusal to allow her to remain with her first foster family. She repeated her regret for this decision and for her subsequent placement in the second foster home. She described the man and woman as miserable people whose only motivation for fostering children was the money. It seems that the husband was at home on permanent disability from a job-related injury. She said that he was always loading and unloading his guns in her presence and that he had made sexual advances towards her. Her complaints to her social worker were not readily acknowledged. This made Jessie frustrated.

She remembered that she had called her worker from

school and described her impressions of the foster father —
his drunkenness, the incident about the picture of the naked
girl, and his obsession with guns. "I guess she was trying to
show me that all men who drank weren't the same as my
father," continued Jessie. "I guess after what happened at
the last foster home, she really didn't take my word for
anything. She thought that I was at fault. I don't think that
she believed me. It's not that she didn't visit the home. She
came up to the trailer and could see the mess and the dishes
in the sink with gook all around. She saw everything
including the guns and still wouldn't believe me. There was
even a guinea pig with junk around. They never cleaned out
the cage. It seems that everything I want, my worker doesn't.
I'm really very hurt by this. And the stuff that I don't want,
she wants for me. She always does the opposite. I think that
she wants to see how far she can go and how much I can
take," Jessie confided.

Jessie's persistence eventually worked in her favor and
she was removed from this foster home. However, she was
still bitter about her relationship with this particular worker.

Jessie then responded to my enquiries about her social
life at the group home. She immediately perked up. Jessie
had struck up a serious relationship with a young 16-year-
old boy who also resided at the home (he was not a
member of the group home since it was not co-ed, but lived
on the campus of the larger residential children's home).
She was in love with him and had dreams of marriage in the
near future. They were kindred spirits. He had had his share
of troubles and was currently traveling around the country
with a wagon train. They planned to marry after her
graduation from high school and after he finds a good job.
Her face lit up for the first time since our meetings. She
became enthusiastic about what she was saying. She said
that she really loved his parents and that she would spend
every weekend with them. Her remarks were interspersed
with giggles.

Jessie relaxed in her chair. It was pleasant watching this
positive transformation. Jessie seemed truly happy about her
future.

I asked her about his problems and how he had come to live at the children's home. "Oh," responded Jessie, "he had behavior problems. Then he turned to drugs. He was smoking pot almost everyday and then he started taking *trips* and he would get angry over little things. When he first came here, he tried to get over his drug problems. He was doing really good for about two to three months and then he started hanging around boys at school who were doing drugs, so he got back on them."

She then continued talking about her future husband by describing some of his prior behavior problems. She continued, "He smashed two of his parents' cars when he was living at home. He threatened to kill them. One time he tried heroin and cocaine and downers, just about everything. He had to go *cold turkey* when he was put in detention. He really got sick over that. He got dizzy and nauseated."

It was then that I posed the question about how he had treated her. Jessie shrugged her shoulders and said that he had never beaten her. When she met him, he wasn't doing drugs except for alcohol.

"He quit when we started going together," said Jessie. "I saw what drugs did to my brother and I know what alcohol does to people and I just don't want to be like that, especially if I have kids."

I interjected my observations about other young people her age. I stated that I had noted that most youngsters in similar circumstances often turn to drugs as a way of coping with their problems. I asked her how she could be so objective about her own situation and how she could be so firm about wanting to avoid drugs in her future family.

She then confirmed my previous hunch about the positive influence that her paternal grandmother had had on her for most of her life. "Well, my grandmother," she said, "always told me to be my own self and don't get wrapped up in what other people are doing. I have always kept this in mind. She's taught me all kinds of things. Lots of my friends have offered me beer and pot. But I wouldn't want to behave like them — go off and do something to hurt somebody else. And I don't like hurting other people. When I found out about my boyfriend's addiction, I decided to help him stay off the drugs," she stated.

I was curious about the reason why she was attracted to him in the first place. She said that he was very nice to her and that they had similar interests. She said that even though he had smashed up cars and destroyed other people's property in the past, she was not afraid of him because he had never hurt anyone.

Jessie continued, "He's never hurt another person. When he was on drugs and when he drinks he bangs up things, not people. I have this feeling that if I lose him, that's gonna be it and I'm gonna hate men forever. Before I came to the home, I used to have this feeling that men weren't worth anything, but then when I started to get close to him, he let me find out that not all men are like my dad or that other foster home father. That really helped me a lot." She was convinced that his time spent with the drug-free wagon train and their separation from each other would help prepare both of them for the responsibilities of marriage.

I continued to probe her fear of possibly hating the opposite sex if things didn't work out between the two of them. She feared that she would end up like her mom or turn out like her social worker (unmarried and bitter).

"All the male friends I have at school just use you. That really turns me off," said Jessie. "All the guys I know have one thing that they care about and it's sex. I haven't met one who isn't like that. I'm just skeptical. I guess my experience with my dad has had a lot to do with the way I feel.

"I really feel special about the kind of thing between my boyfriend and me and I don't want anything to happen to ruin it. He's the first and only guy that I've met that isn't like all the rest of the guys. If I lose him, I don't know.

"When everything was first happening, I was feeling guilty — feeling it was my fault. 'Cause my dad would always say, 'If you weren't a whore, you wouldn't have this problem.' I was really sick of myself. I was so disgusted. I just felt guilty about everything, even taking him to court. I can't blame my mother. She did try to help. I feel that she should leave my father and get help for herself. She doesn't have any experience to support herself. I think that she stays there for the security. She's never moved out of the house — I think she feels that if she moved out my dad would get real angry. He might kill her. You never know. My dad has ways of finding out. He can find out anything. He'd track her down and probably kill her.

"I talked to Mom not long ago, but she doesn't really talk to me anymore. She probably doesn't think of me as a daughter anymore since I reported Dad. I really feel the rejection now. My dad's usually home when I call her. One time he took the phone away from Mom when he heard that she was talking to me. It's been a year and three months since I left home and she still hasn't come round. Nobody's called or visited me, not even any of my brothers. I went back once for a visit with my present caseworker and my sister gave me a big hug and said that she missed me. I think that she's scared to death to contact me on her own.

"Our house is really gettin' worn down. It was in bad shape the last time I was there. My dad must still be gamblin'. And from the looks of Mom's eyes, she's probably still on Valium. When I saw her, she was really shaky. My dad wouldn't look at me — not in the eyes. Whenever I would look at him, he'd turn away. My sister was the only one who was smilin'.

"It's takin' me a year to adjust to bein' away from home. I'm getting used to all of the changes and I'm looking to the future. I'm not really living in the present. I'm thinking about the future. I like being by myself. I can't be that way at the group home. I can't wait to be out on my own. I try to keep smilin' all the time. I used to be very angry all the time, but now it seems that I've got over it. I'm not really happy 'though. I've pretty much accepted what's happened now. I can't change what's happened, so there's not much use to being angry.

"When I was angry, I was moody. I mouthed back at people and I cut school a lot. I made up this big story about bein' cut up by this guy, but I cut myself. I just wanted attention I guess. I used to use four-letter words; now I don't use them so often. Once I realized that I was no longer goin' to live with my family, I began to change. I belived that I should start livin' for myself. I want to go to college and major in a computer related field. The home's gonna look into paying for my education. I used to feel sorry for myself, but I've got over it. I asked my house parent to look into a scholarship for me. I'm thankful for the group home. I didn't know what to expect before I came here. I thought the place would be surrounded by barbed wire and it'd be like a prison. My social worker didn't really prepare me for what was to come. She just said that I would have lots of restrictions so I was very anxious about coming."

Jessie continued to talk in fluent uninterrupted thought sequences about her fears. She stated that her greatest fear was the "fear of not being accepted by people." She continued, "Everybody always seems to be looking down on me. It's pretty scary. I've made friends with two girls from school. But I feel that all the other kids are lookin' down at me. I really feel strange at school. Nobody really talks to me. Back home I was in a much smaller school and so I knew everybody. Now I'm in a big high school. It's so different here. It really bugs me. I usually take a book along with me at lunch. It helps since nobody's gonna talk to me anyway.

"I used to have nightmares after I first came to the house. I used to have them before I came here. I'd wake up screamin' sometimes. There was one nightmare that kept comin' back all the time."

Jessie shared the details, "My sister and I were alone in the house. We had just gone to bed. Mom and Dad weren't home. They had just gone out. And we heard the door open. It was my dad. He had come home without my mom. We asked him where Mom was and he said he had shot her and put her in the river. He seemed to be drunk so we didn't know if we should believe him. And so my sister and I went back to sleep. Then the next thing you know, my dad came into our room and started gettin' after me. I began to scream at him shouting.'No,no, no!' At that point I would wake up screamin."

Jessie also had another nighmare. In it her dad would be beating her dog with a belt and then would turn on her and go after her with the belt. He would hit her across the face with the belt at which point Jessie would wake up screaming. Jessie said that her screams would awaken practically everyone at the home.

One time she had pounded the wall and bruised her fist in the process. Jessie explained that she was fighting off her father's advances. The nightmares lasted over a period of nine months. She said that now that she's convinced that her father can't hurt her anymore, her nightmares occur less frequently and are less intense. Her fear of him has turned to pity.

She continued to talk about her fears. She said that she had always been very concerned on a conscious level about her mother's situation at home and that both she and her sister were always worried about their mom's welfare. They often discussed these concerns. Jessie believed that her father could kill their mom. She and her sister agreed that if their mother were murdered, they would both leave home and establish themselves somewhere else.

"When Dad got very violent, we didn't know what was gonna happen," stated Jessie. This concern was on her mind at all times. Jessie said that she was constantly worried about what she might find when she came home from school or out on a date. She said that she worries less about this ever happening now because of her father's current ill health.

Since her exodus from home, Jessie's father has had serious health problems requiring surgery and hospitalization. This, she feels has had an enormous impact on his ability to carry out his threats of physical violence and has sharply incapacitated him. But for his current medical problems, Jessie would still be plagued by the harping fear of her mother's potential murder. Her father's illness had turned out to be a blessing for the family — for her mother, for her sister and for herself. It seemed to neutralize the anger and anxiety and guilt that was such a familiar part of Jessie's psyche.

"I used to be afraid of growing up," said Jessie. "I used to think that when I grew up, I'd be like my dad." Jessie chuckled as she continued discussing her fears. "I identified more with my dad than with my mom. It still bugs me a little bit now. I was afraid that maybe one day my friends would push me into drinking and I'd like it and that later on after I had kids, I'd hit them and mistreat them. I've read stories about kids who have been abused growing up to hurt their kids who grow up to hit their kids. It's like it's in the genes. I want lots of children so I don't think that I will ever let myself take a drink.

"I feel as though Mom has abandoned me. She really doesn't try to communicate with me. It just hurts me. It seems to me that she has forgotten about the past — buried it. I think that both she and my sister have been brainwashed by my father into not remembering what really has happened and why I'm not home now. I think that if I were to remind my mom about what my dad has done to me and my sister, she would have a stroke and die. This is why I don't really bring up any of the stuff that's happened. I'm afraid that it might kill my mother. I think that my sister is probably afraid that the past might come back if she thinks about it and that it's safer for her to erase the memory of it. She was saying to me last summer that she was having these dreams about when she was 15 years old and that she wanted to go to a psychiatrist, but then she stopped short by stating that dad wouldn't let her.

"I think that my nightmares after I left home helped me because when I awoke and realized that they were only dreams and that Dad wasn't there, I had nothing to be afraid of. I've got used to the idea that my dad is not present. The fact that he is not nearby made the nightmares go away. That was a relief. I've really changed since I've been away from home. I used to be a nervous wreck living at home. When he'd be out, I'd be scared of what he'd do when he came home. I'd sit up and peek through the curtains to see if he'd be comin' in from a drunken binge. There was nothin' really to do at home besides doin' my homework and watchin' TV. It was hard waitin' for him to come home. Sometimes I'd feel like screamin'.

"I used to hate older men, too. It was in my mind that older guys were no good. Everytime I got near my school principal or vice principal I'd shy away. I had a fear of being touched by anybody older. But I'm getting over it. Now that I'm safe at the home, I don't feel as strongly about this. I get really afraid walking down the street at night if there are any guys that I have to pass on the street. I start running and sometimes I stumble over myself trying to get away from them. I'm trying to face my fears now that I'm going to counselling."

I then asked Jessie to try to be as objective as she possible could and explain her father's behavior. She had a great deal of difficulty with this. It was sometime before she could put her feelings into words. "I'd say he had a problem," she paused, "and he shouldn't be gettin' after his daughters." Jessie was at a loss for words. It was next to impossible for her to talk about him.

She then began to talk about her grandmother. She said that her grandmother doesn't know about what her dad has done to her and her sister. She said that she wouldn't want to hurt her with the facts and that she'd probably stop talking to her son if she knew the truth.

"My dad knew what he was doin' to us. A few times he'd wake up and my mom would tell him what he'd done the night before and he'd look shocked. But most of the time he remembered what he had done. He was nice sometimes. This was confusing. I never knew what to expect when he'd come home. This would make all of us edgy. Sometimes he'd come home and not touch me, other times he'd attack me or my sister. It was hard."

Jessie tried hard to understand her father's behavior. But she could not come to terms. "I grew up not being able to trust anybody. My brothers and sisters weren't allowed to have friends over and we weren't allowed to tell anybody about what went on. It was hard keepin' it all in. I learned not to trust anyone because of this. I was never allowed to go to birthday parties and do the things that other kids my age were doin'. It was part of keepin' available for my dad. I went from bein' a child to bein' a grown-up. I think that he tried to make me into somethin' that he had in his imagination. It was as though my sister and I were his creations. I got the impression that even though I was only

a young teenager, he wanted me to be an adult. He'd tell me
to dye my hair blonde. I think that maybe he had an old
girlfriend he was tryin' to make me into. He was strange.
He'd make me do a 'striptease'. Maybe he used to go out
with a stripteaser.

"I think that sometimes he forgot that he was the father
and I was the daughter. When I was 15, he got angry 'cause
I brought my boyfriend home. I thought this would satisfy
him. But he got angry. He knows what he's done." The
conversation was strained at this point. Jessie's voice lacked
enthusiasm. It was tired and weary.

We shifted our conversation to the subject of mothering.
I asked her for her definition of what a mother should be.
She responded that a mother should always give hugs and
kisses to her children because it shows that she cares for
you. The ideal mother would be "someone who's there
when you do something good in school and you can get
praised for it and you don't have to worry about her gettin'
into an argument with your dad. She's also someone who's
strong, not someone who can easily be taken over like my
mom, and someone who can get involved in activities with
you and helps you with them — just somebody who's happy
all the time."

Although Jessie's mom never served as a positive maternal
role model, she felt that her grandmother had served as an
excellent example of what a good mother should be.

"She always gave me a hug and a kiss whenever I went to
her house. I've seen both sides, and I know which is better,"
added Jessie.

Jessie then observed that in addition to her grandmother's
positive influence, her participation in a local church youth
group also helped. Although her father prohibited Jessie
from getting involved in community and school activities,
he rather oddly permitted her this one outlet. Jessie was able
to escape from the perils of living in a violent home by
attending the youth group with some regularity on Sunday
evenings. "At first youth group was just a way of gettin' out
of the house, but then I started to like it. I made some
friends," commented Jessie.

I then asked about her house parents at the group home. I was interested in knowing how they were able to break through the years of distrust and personal anguish and what problems, if any, she had had in adjusting to the new living situation. She responded in the following way, "I think the house-parents feel that we've missed something in our life and they're trying to put it back in even though it's a little late. They're just trying to make us all feel like we're part of one big family as they call it here. They don't mean to treat us like children. Every once in a while they'll say, 'no', if we want to go somewhere because they're thinking like a mother. I used to think that they were treating me like a child because they wouldn't let me do half the stuff I wanted to do, but then I realized that had I done some of those things, I might have got into trouble and it wouldn't have been in my best interest. I used to get so mad, but one night I sat down and wrote down what I would have done in their position and I came up with the same solutions as theirs. When I first came here, I felt that I was being treated like a ten-year-old. But I think that they were trying to show me that they really cared and that they wanted to protect me. I felt that even though I was living someplace different, there were people who could care about me. This is good."

We then continued to discuss her positive feelings and thoughts about her group home placement which was the turning point of her life. It was for her the beginning of the beginning. It was her first encounter with justice, reason, security, tenderness, responsibility, caring and trust. While at the group home, Jessie felt protected from the hardcore violence and molestation of her real home. The house parents became her surrogate parents, who taught her to believe in other people, but more importantly, to believe in herself. It was a place for her to grow in self-confidence and to mollify her fears. It was where she had begun the process of self-examination and where she was learning to shed the layers of crippling guilt over her relationship with her disturbed father. It was a necessary transition between violence and sanity.

Jessie benefited from the small family-like infrastructure

of the group home. It prepared her for her eventual placement with foster parents and reduced the risk of having it end in failure. The group home gave her stability. It served to create inner strength by enabling Jessie to draw upon her positive inner resources without having to worry about adjusting to the pressures of a new foster mother and father.

Jessie and I began discussing a hypothetical situation. I asked her what she would do if the man she was married to started to drink and then became abusive to her daughters. She answered, "I'd probably move out and take my daughters with me. I'd let him come to terms with what he had done. If not, I'd never see him again. I would have to be careful about who I pick as a husband because it would really be my fault if I chose the wrong man. I wouldn't want that to happen. If somebody would treat me rotten, and be a womanizer I wouldn't stay with him. My boyfriend drinks but he's not the type to beat me up. I guess you could call it instinct. I can tell. I would be very cautious about drinking since my dad has that problem. Also guys who can't express their feelings shouldn't be trusted. My boyfriend is very open with me, so I don't think that he'd be a problem."

I asked her to use her imagination and tell me what advice she would give to an imaginary daughter. "My advice," she said, "is that you shouldn't rush into anything. Make sure that he doesn't drink too much and watch out for guys who treat you bad. I plan to tell my daughter what happened to me so that she can watch out for men in the world. I think that my boyfriend would make a good father. I've seen him working with little kids and he gets along with his little brothers and sisters. Even when he drinks, he acts okay with his mother and the rest of the family."

I then asked her if she would ever consider returning to her home. She said probably not because she'd been away so long and because she gets along so well with her boyfriend's family. She spends the holidays with them. They've become like family to her. She said that spending time with them has enabled her to "come to the conclusion that all parents aren't bad". Even though her boyfriend has had major problems, she's been able to observe what it's like for parents who care. She's seen them get thoroughly involved in his recovery. She's learned to appreciate their sense of concern and their genuine love for their son. This realization has played a major role in her own recovery process. As far as her dad is concerned, she knows that she could never go back home for more than an hour.

Jessie knew that her relationship with her father could not ever be totally mended, but she hoped and prayed that someday in the future their differences would be reconciled. I left Jessie that day feeling more hopeful about her circumstances that I had ever been.

There were a number of things in her favor: her placement in a group home for girls, her educational endeavors and her recent serious relationship with a boyfriend whom she planned to marry, her productive visits with his parents and her paternal grandmother's significant influence as a strong and independent woman. I began to think about what could have been her fate if just one of the above variables did not funnel into her life experience.

If grandmother had died before Jessie's birth, or if she lived far away, or if she lacked strength of character, where would Jessie be today? If the group home was crowded and she was forced to stay at home or reside in an institutional facility, or if she were placed with another set of inappropriate foster parents, where would Jessie be today? If she had not met a young man whom she could trust and dream about the future, where would Jessie be today? If his parents weren't open and understanding and caring people, where would Jessie be today?

I met with Jessie several months after our initial meetings. She was bubbling over with excitement. For the first time since we had met Jessie seemed truly happy. "Well," I said, "I can't wait to hear what's been happening since our last talk."

Jessie beamed, "I might be goin' into a foster home. If things work out, I'll be leavin' here in about two weeks. I've always wanted to see what a normal family is like. Now I'll get my chance." Jessie continued, "I'm so happy. I got my wish."

She said that she had met with the foster parents the night

before and she was really looking forward to living with
them. They have two of their own children. Jessie said that
she got a "good first impression of the parents." She could
hardly wait to meet the children. Jessie described the couple
as being in their late thirties. They lived on a farm. I told her
that she looked very happy.

"Do you think that this might be it?" I asked.

"Yeh! Yeh!" she replied.

Jessie was breathless at the possibility of having her
dream come true. She said that the family seems to be able
to communicate with each other. "That's the first thing that
got my attention. They're just different from any people I've
ever met before," she continued. "They're goin' to help me
to get my permit so I can drive one of their spare cars. I feel
relieved 'cause now I know where I'm headed for, I don't
feel so uncertain about my life. And I'm happy. I'm very
excited. I'm gonna try hard to make this work," said Jessie.

I asked her how she would react to any disagreements or
misunderstandings that might arise between her and the
new foster parents. I was concerned that she might run away
again. She responded, "Living at the home has been an
advantage. I've learned how to deal with my anger. I used to
leave whenever I got angry or I used to punch walls. Now
I've learned to sit down and talk to the person I'm angry at
or to talk to somebody else about it until I cool down. So,
I've learned how to handle that. Before I didn't know what
to do except leave. I've always left home or when I was
younger, I withdrew into a little corner and stayed by myself
whenever I was angry. When I was living at home I couldn't
tell anybody how angry I was. There was nobody to listen.
My dad was allowed to show his anger without anybody
questionin' it. But when anybody else got angry, we weren't
expected to show it. If we did, we would be punished," said
Jessie. "My dad didn't think we had the right to be angry."

I asked Jessie to tell me how she was different now. She
said that when she first arrived at the group home, she was
quiet and subdued. A couple of times when she had words
with the other girls at the home she would leave at night or
punch walls. It was through her counselling sessions at the

group home that her responses to anger began to be shaken and changes started to occur.

"I learned that I wasn't facing my problems. I was running away from them instead. At first I didn't want to listen to this explanation, but finally it dawned on me. I needed to stay and work out my problems and not run away. It took a long time for me to accept this, but when I did, everything began to fall into place. I tried it when a girl picked a fight with me because she took some clothes of mine without askin'. Instead of yellin' and screamin' at her, I said, 'Let's sit down and talk this out.' We talked it over and I said that she should ask me if she wanted anything and I'd loan it to her. And it worked. I learned that staying and workin' it out is better than not facin' up to it.

"I also learned that talkin' things out made me feel good. When I'd get angry about somethin', I felt that I could always talk to one of the house parents. They would be there to listen to me and when I finished telling them what was bothering me, I'd always feel a lot better. This helped me a lot. Before coming here, everything use to build up inside of me until finally I'd explode. It's important to talk about things right away and not let them stay inside you so you don't one day all of a sudden do somethin' terrible."

Jessie had learned two important lessons about dealing with her anger. She learned that she should not deny it, that she should face up to it and accept it. Second, she learned what to do with it once resigned to it. She learned the value of converting her anger, which had heretofore been physically and violently expressed, to the spoken word. She was able to say that she was angry, why she was angry, and finally, to discuss possible ways of solving her problems.

Then Jessie said something remarkable, "Things that used to bother me don't seem that important anymore. I find that I laugh a lot more instead of gettin' upset." Jessie laughed, "It seems funny that I used to get angry over most things. I feel that things can usually be worked out. There are big things and small things. There are some things that are worth getting angry about, but there are others that just deserve a laugh."

Jessie had gained perspective. She had learned to evaluate her own feelings and to separate out and identify many different emotions. Everything was not just black and white to her. There weren't only two states of being for her — angry and non-angry. For Jessie a whole new world of feelings had become a part of her working emotional vocabulary. She was able to say that she was happy or sad or angry or frightened or depressed or frustrated or hurt or nervous or lonely or jealous or guilty, etc., and that conflict did not have to lead to the vicious cycle of violence. She learned that there were many choices of reaction. Jessie was able to feel good about discovering these myriad choices. This realization, in turn, was positive reinforcement for continuing to behave in such a manner.

In short, she had learned that anger is but one of many negative emotions and that it need not necessarily lead to acts of violence. As such, she was able to achieve a balance between feelings and reactions. She was no longer confined to a two-step solution approach, viz, anger-violence. Instead her universe of possible choices and alternatives had expanded, enabling Jessie to view herself as a person with unlimited possibilities and choices.

She said that if any problems arise between her and her new foster parents, she intends to discuss them, rather than "do something irrational".

"I've learned," she continued, "the hard way how to deal with anger."

She felt comfortable knowing that the group home would be available to help if necessary. But she was committed to investing all of her resources into making the new placement a success. She expressed confidence in her own ability to discharge anger without destroying herself or the relationship in the process. "I've learned to trust myself," she repeated with new found confidence.

I asked her if she felt any conflict about "giving up her biological family for the foster family." She responded, "As far as my natural family goes, I feel like an outsider. Even if I tried to take my sister away from the house, I'd feel sorry that my mom wouldn't have anyone left that she could talk to. And I'm just hoping (I know that this sounds far from reality) that my dad will change so I can go home and visit without worrying about feeling fear or guilt about leaving him. I think it was smart for me to have spoken to my school counselor in the first place. If I hadn't, I probably still would have been living at home, pale and skinny and depressed and possibly on drugs. Now I feel healthy and I don't have to worry about what would happen from one day to the next with my dad. Even though it hurt to leave, I think if I would have stayed there, I might have even tried suicide or somethin'".

She then spoke about an arrangement that she had worked out with her new foster parents, allowing her to visit with her boyfriend's parents every other weekend. She was delighted about this because she felt so close to them and really looked forward to seeing them on a regular basis. Her advice to other teenage girls who might be in similar circumstances was "to talk to somebody and get help to work out the problem. If they can't work it out, then the next best thing is to get out of the situation."

I then asked her to pretend for the moment that she was a featured speaker at a local high school and that she was to address an audience of teenage boys and girls about the subject of family violence. I instructed her to think about how she might present the topic without making the students feel uncomfortable. She said that coincidentally she had just completed and presented a report about child abuse to her class and that she made it very factual instead of personal. She told them about its possible causes.

"One girl asked me if I thought that spankings were child abuse. I told her that not always, and that child abuse is a very delicate situation and difficult to really understand what makes the parents do it — that sometimes inside they don't really mean to hurt the children, but that sometimes they can't help themselves," said Jessie.

She continued, "One guy told the class about a man who took a baby and swung its head around. It hit the ground and died. And then other kids in the class started gettin' into more examples and different stories that they knew about.

They asked me to tell them about my own experiences. I tried to but I had to sit down 'cause I couldn't talk about it anymore.

"After my report, another girl gave a report about child abuse and she started emphasizing that it's usually the kid's fault and not the parents. Then everybody started to argue about what she was sayin'. They were confused. But the teacher interrupted and said that since I had had personal experience, the class should believe me. She said that people don't usually get involved if they know someone is being abused. I felt that she was right on target 'cause my neighbors heard screamin' comin' from our house and they never called the cops or reported it. I think that teenagers have a general idea about what child abuse is. It's just that they're very unsure about the emotional and psychological effects. They tend to think that it's just a matter of physical beatings and that's all there is to it. They don't know about the whole picture."

No one could possibly truly know what Jessie's personal tragedy had been. No one could feel all of the pain of rejection, the degradation of sexual abuse, the fear of murder and suicide, the distrust of humanity, the doubting of her own sanity. All that we as human beings with a capacity to reach out and help can do is to give the Jessies in our society a second chance at life by not judging her, by being compassionate and understanding, and by encouraging her to believe in herself. These goals can be accomplished but not without the appropriate community resources and not without carefully trained and sensitized professionals who recognize the benefits to the individuals and to the society at large.

CHAPTER 6

Real Mad

"I remember some stuff. Like I remember I punched somebody, but I didn't remember who. I didn't remember who I was fightin' and I didn't know for how long or where. I knew it was in school, but I didn't know which room it was in."

David, a 13-year-old schoolboy with dirty blonde hair, fair complexion and a trace of a southern drawl spoke freely about his frequent altercations with his peers and sometimes with adults. He was a polite, well-spoken young boy. I had to coax him at first to speak up so that I could hear him better — he seemed a bit shy, but not hostile or unfriendly. He soon warmed up to me and we had, what I felt to be, lively and revealing discussions regarding his remarkable family history.

He was living at home with his mother and three stepsisters, two of whom were younger than he. His older stepsister was the product of a previous marriage between his mother and a man whom David had never known. He had never really known his biological father very well since

he left David's mother when David was too young to
remember anything significant. He would visit his dad who
had since remarried, but his new stepmother did not want
David visiting with them. He was quite emphatic about this.

"His wife said that they'd move out if I went down to see
them again," said David. He continued, "She keeps writing
nasty letters to my mom and me." His younger stepsisters
were born to David's mother and her third husband, who
she had since divorced. David's life with his mother and
stepsisters was far from tranquil. He confided that his
mother had a problem with her temper and that during the
course of his childhood she had had difficulty with her
"nerves". He seemed to think that his mom and her third
husband had separated because of fights between them and
that she was physically abused by him. He was living in a
very tense and always chaotic atmosphere at home. David
described his mother as a very tall blonde woman in her
mid-thirties with shoulder length hair. They didn't seem to
have much of a relationship together. He spoke about the
great rift in communication between them.

His mother was the victim of numerous nervous breakdowns. David described those episodes as periods of great
solitude when his mother would literally shut herself off
from her children and bury herself on the sofa in book after
book. There were times when she would not bathe or
perform any of the usual household chores. She would sit
spellbound immersed in the fantasy world of fiction or
biography untouched by the ordinary needs of four growing
youngsters. During those bouts David and his sisters were
forced to run the household without adult supervision. He
would cook supper and sometimes help his sisters with the
dusting. These extra responsibilities bothered him less than
his concern over his mother's bizarre behavior pattern. She
was known to fly into uncontrollable acts of rage and David
was the usual target. He felt he was treated unfairly and
resented being blamed for everything that didn't suit his
mother.

His mother's breakdowns often required her to be
hospitalized for long periods, at which time David and his

stepsisters stayed with friends of his mother or more recently in individual foster homes. He revealed that usually before her hospitalizations, his mother's behavior would become dangerously violent. Prior to his last foster placement, his mother came very close to annihilating both of them in an unsuccessful attempt at murder/suicide which was accidentally aborted by the arrival of an assigned visiting homemaker who had stopped by the house to offer her assistance on that infamous day.

The events of that near fatal day for David were a constant source of stress and anxiety to him. About five weeks after the incident, he had learned from his foster parents that his mom was going to be released from the hospital. David panicked at the news. He could not bear having to return to the custody of his unstable mother. He was terrified by what had recently transpired between them and could not face a reunion under any circumstances. David longed to remain in the care of his foster parents and their normal family. The specter of being removed from their safe and secure home completely unnerved him. Instead of discussing his fears with his foster parents, he bottled them up. "I usually hold stuff in and then when one thing ticks me off, I let it all out," confided David. Unfortunately for David, he exploded one day during an argument with his 17-year-old foster brother whom he was verbally taunting and harassing. His foster brother was trying to complete his physics homework and David kept interrupting and teasing him. One thing led to another. What had started out as a verbal assault ended in a physical collision between the two of them. David lost control and broke anything he could get his hands on. Curtains were pulled down, furniture was thrown, audio tapes were unwound and papers were scattered around the room. His foster parents ran downstairs to their basement bedroom to break up the struggle. David admitted that his "mind blacked out during the fight and I could punch my fist through the wall and not even feel it until I calm down." David's foster parents were alarmed at what they had witnessed. They felt that David needed professional help and that they were not capable of handling him and his violent temper without outside intervention.

"I didn't remember anything," said David. "Like last year I got into a fight with a teacher and I got suspended for five days for assault and battery 'cause I punched her in the jaw. My mind blacked out. I was told later that I was fighting with this kid in my class who had got me in a head lock. I didn't know that my teacher had come up behind me. I thought it was another kid who always bothers me and so I thought I'd teach him a lesson. Only it was my teacher who got punched. I apologized to her later on. When somebody gets me real mad, there's no tellin' what I'm gonna do."

David's foster parents explained that they were "scared" and that they felt he should spend some time away from them getting better. They called him at school to inform him that he wouldn't be returning to their home for a while and reassured him that his placement in a residential home for children for "testing" purposes would be a temporary arrangement. David felt confident that he would be remanded back to the foster family. He was grateful to them for "surprising" him with the news at school, otherwise he surely would have run away.

"I figured they told me over the phone so I wouldn't get mad and run away and have the cops after me. They were right 'cause I would have took off," said David. "They want me to learn some rules. I'll be adjusted to the rules here, but I'm not so sure that when I go back home I'll be adjusted to the rules at their home. Here I'm very surprised. It's not the same in a regular home situation. I figure that maybe they should have kept me home and arranged for me to see a guidance counselor maybe two to three times a week while I was still livin' with them. Then I think I could learn how to adjust to their rules quicker and better," David reflected.

His observation was very sensible and quite astute for a boy of 13 years. He indicated that he was aware of a plan to reintegrate him with his foster parents, which included regular weekly sessions with a family counselor. David felt quite comfortable knowing that both he and the family would be able to work out their problems within a natural setting. He did not relish being separated from them again in the future. He said that prior to his placement in a home for children, he feared what might lay ahead.

"I didn't know what it was going to be like. I didn't know whether I was going to be gettin' into fights every five seconds. Was my food going to be stolen right from under my face? I didn't know what to expect, so I just did what everybody else did," said David. He expressed feelings of doubt and trepidation that are common to most children who find themselves suddenly removed from their familiar surroundings. He disliked his current situation enough to want to cooperate with his assigned therapist, social worker and school teacher so that he could hasten his return to foster care.

David and I then began to discuss what he termed "blackouts", which he said he experienced everytime he would be involved in a fist fight with another person.

"When I fight, there's only one thing on my mind, 'get him; get him and get away'," David stated. He said that he always had a great deal of difficulty remembering the details of each fight immediately afterwards. He speculated that the reason for this lapse of awareness could be because "I get scared."

"In fourth grade I got suspended 13 times in one year for hitting other kids and startin' fights," continued David. But he was never able to recall the specifics. His main focus was on destroying his opponent. He was able to channel all of his energies into achieving this one important goal — his adversary's destruction. He had become single-minded in this pursuit. To that end David admitted that he would stop at nothing. Once enmeshed in the physcial confrontation, David could not of his own volition wrest himself from the struggle. He would, as he put it, "lose control". He was unable to disengage without external intervention. This meant that David was prepared to fight until he was reasonably sure that he had won the battle.

When he reasoned that his blackouts originated because he was "scared", David was alluding to his vulnerability as a child who had frequently witnessed violent confrontations between his mother and her third husband and who had been the selected target of his mother's physical abuse after the divorce. He had observed his mother's unharnessed rage — and was too little and too powerless to protect himself from her uncontrolled wrath. He mentioned that his older stepsister had similar problems and that both of them would often get involved in fist fights with the neighbor's children. David was a frightened child. He had learned at a very early age that there was no middle ground. That once the fighting began, you fought to the finish and you won.

David's youth was spent in learning that there was no place in his world of survival for verbal disagreements, for compromise, for negotiation. These concepts were foreign to him. His life was constantly being challenged at home, so he believed that any assult on him (by his mother or by a peer) was a threat to his very survival. He reacted to all conflicts with the same response — uncontrolled rage.

His fear ("I was scared") of death combined with conditioning to react with violence fueled his infinite source of blind rage. What he was doing, when he was doing it, even why he was doing it were irrelevant. To David, winning, surviving, staying alive were paramount. All else in his mind became trivial and therefore insignificant so not worth remembering. And, thus, the blackouts.

There is also another possible explanation for the explosive rage followed by blackouts. Dr. Frank A. Elliott offers a neurological perspective in his article "The Neurology of Explosive Rage: The Dyscontrol Syndrome".[69] Dr. Elliott addresses the possibility of organic rather than psychogenic origin when the following criteria are met:

1. A family history of violent attacks of rage (spanning several generations) — he notes that in such families it is often difficult to determine if the cause is purely organic in nature or if it is due to emotional trauma or modeling or a combination of both since violent rage tends to create dissension, chaos and instability in families where one member suffers from the disorder.

2. Dr. Elliott divides his patients into two groups:
   a. Symptoms noted during infancy and early child-hood in the form of temper tantrums and contin-

uing into adolescence and adulthood as explosive rage, due to either pre-natal, natal, or postnatal events, such as foetal anoxia or convulsions.

b. Sequela of explosive rage in patients otherwise normal prior to brain injury or metabolic disorder of which various forms of hypoglycemia is most common.

3. Inter-ictal attacks of explosive rage with no amnesia.

4. Inter-ictal attacks of rage which culminate in a convulsion.

The purpose of presenting Dr. Elliott's findings is to point out the need for a comprehensive differential diagnosis in cases of explosive rage so as to determine the appropriate course of treatment management for each individual.

In David's case, he did not have a neurological workup and there was no information in his case history indicating that one was being considered. There was no information regarding birth history so it is impossible to ascertain whether or not there was neurological involvement. Suffice it to say that in such cases where there is a possibility for psychogenic and organic symptoms to coexist, it is advisable to prescribe a series of electroencephalography. It may be that a combination of psychiatric and neurological supervision will best serve the needs of such a patient.

Why David, his mother and his older stepsister exhibitied uncontrollable rage is a crucial question. It would clarify the etiology of their violent disorder and hasten the efficacy of the treatment process. David's case shall, therefore, remain inconclusive as far as source of origin is concerned because all possible determinants had not been ruled out.

David continued to talk about his older stepsister describing her as extremely aggressive, "fightin' and punchin' kids and teachers."

Her violent behavior pattern seemed very similar to David's. However, his younger stepsisters were the antithesis of their older stepsiblings. David said they were "goody two shoes". That the younger children could co-exist within the same family constellation and yet not demonstrate the negative assaultive behaviors of their mother and their elders was also an interesting feature of this family's pathology.

David did not talk at length about his docile younger stepsisters. His grimacing and sarcastic remarks during his brief discussion implied a deep-seated hostility and resentment which I did not choose to investigate. Rather, we explored the topic of his relationship with his mother which had had a more direct effect upon his behavior of late. He characterized their relationship as "we had good times, we had bad times; mostly bad times. Sometimes just we two would go to the mall together — walk around. We'd ride our bikes. But she had an operation on her hand, can't work the hand controls, so we had to get rid of her ten-speeder. So we couldn't go down to the mall much. Lots of times, though, I'd get into a lot of arguments with my younger sisters, and that would get my mom mad and she'd come up and punch me and I'd have to go into my bedroom. She'd always blamed me for all of the fights. Mom beat me for so long with the belt, it doesn't bother me any more. She's been hittin' with a belt ever since I was little. She'd double-fold it. The last time she used a belt on me was about two years ago when she got me in the face. I took the belt and threw it out the window after that. But she found another way to beat me. She started usin' a two by four on my rear. It didn't hurt 'cause I got beat so much I just felt ouch, ouch, ouch, ouch, and no pain. Never had a black eye, but I did have bruises over my body. When she found out I was playin' with fire crackers, she held my hand over the gas stove and burned my hand. She just said, 'Too bad.' It took five weeks to heal. I told everybody at school that I got hurt by fallin' off my bike. She threw me down the stairs once when I was six. She pushed me. I fell into the living room and hit a chair. I thought to myself, 'Boy, this is fun.' "

David then described his mother's most recent break-down and the events which preceded his most recent removal from the home. "She aimed a gun at me," David blurted in a detached matter of fact style. It was no more remarkable to him than if she had pointed a finger at him. David inured himself to bear the threatening acts of violence that his mother had repeatedly committed against him.

I asked David why his mother had done this. He said that she was extremely upset because he had defied her directive to take a particular route home from school. He decided to take a shortcut instead of heeding his mother's wishes. The decision inconvenienced his mother who was supposed to meet him along the specified route so that they could ride to a doctor's appointment together. When she couldn't connect with him, she drove home in a fury and entered David's room.

After David explained that he had walked through the park instead of taking the other longer route, David said, "She pushed back her jacket and she had a gun. She asked me, 'Are you gonna walk that way again? I told you I didn't want you walkin' that way.' I said, 'No.' She said that she was gonna kill me, then herself. It was a loaded handgun. I was scared at the time. I froze. We were there about 15 minutes. Then my big sister came runnin' upstairs because someone was at the door. It was the lady homemaker who visits us sometimes. If this lady hadn't shown up, Mom would have killed us both. One of my younger sisters is mentally retarded and handicapped and this homemaker used to come over to help my mother out."

I asked David what had happened next. Did he run to the homemaker for help? He said that although he had wanted to be rescued, he chose to retreat to his room instead. He figured that he could jump out of the bedroom window in order to escape if his mother pulled a gun on him again. "Besides," he said, "the homemaker lady might have thought that I was jokin' and not believe me, and maybe my mom would get upset or scared and then hold her hostage with the rest of us. I didn't want to endanger her life, too.

"My mom was the one who told the lady about the gun incident. And then the lady asked me if it was true. That's when I told her it was. Child Welfare came in and took all of us with the cops and my mother was taken to a hospital in an ambulance. They took my mom away. I think that it could happen again. I'm scared to go home. I thought that if I didn't go back to live with my mom, she might ignore me and put me out of her life for good. But my mom told me that she wants me to be happy and she won't hold it against me if I don't go back with her. So I've decided to stay in foster care."

David was pleased with these arrangements. He looked forward to the immediate future when he would be reunited with his foster parents and their children. He was relieved that he could make the choice, knowing that his natural mother would not hold his decision against him. He would have made the choice to remain away from his family of origin, his mother's approval not withstanding. But her good wishes freed him from any guilt feelings that may otherwise have ensued.

David commented about his newly acquired skill of postponing anger in order to quickly defuse a potentially volatile situation. He claimed credit for mastering this technique during his placement at the children's home. He was forced to learn to rely on "crutches" to distract him from an immediate instinctive response to a provocative stimulus. He explained that in order to survive the experience of group living in an environment that could oftentimes be hostile, he had developed a self-imposed delay reaction survival pattern, which included walking away from a fight with a fellow resident, taking a walk around the home's grounds, never verbally responding to a resident when he felt very angry but holding back that first negative impulse.

David indicated that he was able to carry over this discipline to his foster family. He cited a recent example. On his weekend visit with his foster family he was feeling upset about having to return to the institutional home on Sunday evening. He started to express his dismay by becoming argumentative with the various foster family members. However, before he lost control, he was able to step back and consciously decide to choose to use a household "crutch". David asked his foster parents if he could go for a bike ride around the neighborhood instead of remaining in close proximity of them and their children. He realized that by physically removing himself from their presence, he would greatly reduce his chances of getting involved in a violent altercation at a time when his emotions about separation from them were running high.

This was a turning point in his previously explosive behavioral history. David was able to teach himself one of the first lessons of interpersonal conflict management — he taught himself to voluntarily disengage himself from a dispute situation. This lesson was significant. It demonstrated that David would be an excellent candidate for individual or supervised group self-help counselling. Family therapy had been prescribed upon his return to the foster family. However, it would be equally imperative for David to receive specific counselling related to altering his assaultive behavior. Unfortunately, there are no known self-help programs for aggressive and violent adolescent males and females. Such programs would help to insure the success of conventional therapies by emphasizing the role of personal responsibility and consequences, and identifying and communicating feelings.

He was reasonably optimistic about his future life and demonstrated an amazing capacity to rise above his past experiences with a firm commitment to begin the change process with himself. He indicated that he was feeling relieved since he had been removed from his biological mother's care. The greatest stress inducer for him was his mother's possession of the handgun, which she had recently used to threaten him. He feared that his mother would use the gun again if she would suffer another breakdown. He said that he had mixed feelings about the incident and that this was another form of stress for him. On the one hand, he feared for his life; on the other hand, he did not want to say or do anything to jeopardize or harm his mother.

David was very enthusiastic about his foster family. He was happy for the opportunity to live in a normal family setting complete with mother, father, brothers and a dog. He had always missed having a consistent father figure at home — the foster placement was, to David, the realization of a dream for a caring stable father. David described his foster father as a "kind man who doesn't have a problem with his temper and who takes me fishing sometimes." He wanted to witness how "normal folks get along — what they do when they get mad, and how they treat each other."

He felt that he could learn some valuable lessons about settling disagreements without flying into a rage. David's father and stepfather had not been positive role models. His natural father was absent for most of his childhood. The few instances when he'd visit with him were fraught with rejection. He remembers when his stepfather used to fight with his mother and push and shove her while he shouted out curse words.

We further explored his feelings at which point David revealed that he harbored a great deal of anger towards his mother and the way he chose to deal with these sentiments was to block them from coming to the surface. He felt that chances of improving his relationship with his mother were extremely remote and that this factor caused him to feel upset. He was best able to cope with this reality by avoiding close contact with his mother, and by trying not to dwell on the recent past. Most of his thoughts had turned to the new life that lay ahead of him.

We concluded our interview sessions with David expressing his expectations for a future that had great potential for happiness. The prognosis in this case was definitely very hopeful provided, of course, that he and his foster parents receive the benefit of supportive counselling services. David's history was a terribly troubled one. It would be folly to expect positive results without the benefit of professional guidance, particularly for setbacks (which are bound to occur from time to time) and minor crises (which have a tendency to escalate into major problems if left unattended).

CHAPTER 7

Haunted

"I was only three at the time, but I can remember it as if it happened yesterday. I'll never forget it either." These thoughts were uttered by Doreen, a lovely mature-looking 14-year-old. She continued to speak, "My dad used to lock me and my brother in our room all day long. He was out of a job and my mom was out workin' during the day. He kept us in our room so he could do drugs and drink downstairs. He never did nothin' for us while my mom was gone. If we called him for any reason, he'd come in and beat us up with a belt. I'll never forget it. You don't forget bein' locked up from mornin' 'til night that easily." Doreen took a drag on her cigarette. She chain-smoked during the entire interview. She had been smoking for the past two years. She said that it helped to calm her nerves.

Doreen had vivid memories of her addicted father, who she described as violent and abusive. She recalled an incident that occurred when she was only four years old. It involved her mother who, Doreen stated, was his other constant victim of abuse. Her father would usually come home from a night of drinking (which was likely to occur on a daily basis), storm into the bedroom and pick a fight with Doreen's mother. There would always be cursing and obscenities and loud shouts. Doreen remembers one skirmish in particular. It was significant because when the dust settled, Doreen found her mother in bed covered with blood and writhing in pain. Her nose had been broken, her eyes blackened and several ribs broken. She was hospitalized for a three-month period, requiring Doreen and her brother to take up temporary residence with her maternal grandmother.

Shortly after that incident, and when Doreen's mother had fully recovered, her parents divorced. Doreen's maternal uncles beat her father up and physically threw him out of the house immediately after they learned about the assault. Her father heeded their warning never again to return to the house by moving out of state and remarrying shortly after the divorce. Doreen had almost no contact with him after his swift departure, but she could never be released from the flashbacks — the constant and frequent instant replays of her father's hideous attacks on her mother, her brother and herself. The mere mention of his name would trigger the images in her mind. In the ten years since her father's banishment, his memory continued to have a disturbing effect on her.

At 14, Doreen was not able to separate herself from the haunting memories of her early childhood. Although not now physically a threat, her father was a constant source of pain, resentment, fear and sorrow. Doreen's life was touched deeply and traumatically by her early exposure to child and wife abuse. She had never recovered from the dual role of witness and victim, a function which was to have a profound effect on her emotional growth and maturation.

Doreen's mother remarried. Doreen did not have kind words for her stepfather, who constantly beat her and her brother. He did not, however, assault her mother. He was harsh and argumentative with her, but Doreen said, "He never laid a hand on her." During the course of the second marriage, Doreen and her family were in constant flux, moving from a house trailer to three or four apartments.

When she was eight years of age, her mother placed her and her brother in foster care. She said that her mother and stepfather could not financially support them. They remained in foster care for four years, at which time Doreen was returned to her mother's custody. During her placement, Doreen's mother and stepfather were divorced. She was 12 years old when she was reunited with her mother. The intervening years had taken their toll on her mother. Doreen could hardly recognize her mother. She said that her mother was a very different person. Doreen was bewildered by the transformation.

Doreen found her mother dependent on alcohol. "There wasn't a day when she was sober," recalled Doreen. "I started goin' downhill after that. My grades dropped and I kept gettin' in trouble at school. I'd look at my mom and see what she had become and I'd keep seein' the picture of her that night when my real dad had beat her up and I'd get real depressed," confided Doreen.

"I never wanted to tell any of my friends about my mom's drinking problem — never wanted any of my friends to come over. It got so bad — my mom couldn't take care of us anymore. One mornin' she called social services. A caseworker showed up. She knocked on the door. But I didn't want to leave, so I started hollerin' at her and told her to leave. Then I ran into the bathroom. I was tryin' to get out of the bathroom window, but I couldn't so I had to open the door and leave with the social worker. My grandmother was supportin' us during that time and she was gettin' sick of it, so my mom had to give us up.

"I stayed in the foster home for about five months before I was kicked out. When I was livin' with my mom, I had no supervision. I was used to goin' out all night, stayin' with my friends. My foster family didn't know what to do with me, but they were nice. This was during the summer. I got arrested for breakin' curfew. My friends and I were sittin' outside a firehouse. All of a sudden cops came by and arrested us for bein' out past curfew (11:30 p.m.). That's when my foster parents gave up on me.

My foster mom came down to get me — she wasn't mad,

just disappointed, I guess. So I went to live with my grandparents, but they couldn't put up with me. They never let me out. Then I got suspended for smokin' in school. My grandmother came to the school and called me a 'stupid fool'. That's when I grabbed my books and took off. I stayed about a month at my boyfriend's house. My mom paid his mother for my expenses, and then I went back to live with my mom in an apartment. I used to cut school and get high at my mom's. She didn't say nothin' about it."

Doreen began to discuss her problem with substances. It started when she was 12 years old (about the time she had been returned to her mother's custody). She started experimenting with pot and beer. By age 14, Doreen was supporting her drug habit by "dealin' drugs". Her friends were equally involved with drugs, most of them coming from single-parent households with little or no supervision.

Doreen admitted that when she was living with her mother, she never ate right and got tired of running around, keeping late hours. She then arranged during the following summer to stay with a young couple whom she had known for some time. They had two children and agreed to exchange room and board for babysitting and "all the speed I wanted". But she did not stay with them very long. It was about this time that she entered a drug counselling program which was recommended by a caseworker. During the time of the interview, Doreen was drug free. She praised the counselling program for her short-term success and said that she was feeling less depressed about her situation than she had felt before undergoing therapy.

Her depression was at its peak immediately prior to professional intervention. She recalled a recurring disturbing nightmare. The nightmare terrified her. She said that she had a strong sense of someone (she was unable to distinguish whether or not the person was male or female) attempting to suffocate her. There was a sensation of being covered with bed sheets until she couldn't breathe. She would always wake up feeling scared, lonely and crying — not really knowing if the vivid nightmare was a dream or reality. It usually took several minutes for her to regain composure and for the level of anxiety to subside. Doreen attributed these nightmares to her state of depression and to her recent preoccupation with her mother's physical and mental condition.

She said that she felt sorry because her mother's life had been so tough. She blamed her father for ruining her mother's life.

"He caused her a lot of unhappiness. He used to beat her up — at one time he chased her with a knife. I was in my bedroom at the time. She ran into the street screaming for help because he was going to kill her," remarked Doreen. "The neighbors called the police — they arrested him. Mom didn't press charges. She was afraid of what might happen to her after he got of out of jail." Doreen felt that her mother's drinking problem was a direct effect of the beatings. "I think that she drank to forget what he did to her." She said that she was angry with her father and fatalistic about her mother. ("She'll probably be this way for the rest of her life".) She said that she resented her mom for sticking her into all those homes.

"I hate her, but I also love her," commented Doreen. "This makes me angry and frustrated. She knows how much I hate her, but she still goes ahead and puts me into homes. If she keeps on doing this, I'm gonna have to run away," Doreen stated with conviction. "I know that her life has been rotten and that my dad is the cause of her drinkin' and everything, but I still feel mad about what she has done to my life. I hate my dad. When I see my mom drunk, I remember all the beatings that my father gave her and then I start to feel bad about myself."

Doreen was torn between her anger and hatred for her mother and her tremendous sympathy for her. The conflict surfaced shortly after their reunion, following four years of separation, but had recently come to a head when Doreen was placed in a residential home for children. She felt that this was "the last straw". Doreen felt rejected, but most of all, she felt trapped and powerless. Her intellectual understanding of her mother's motivation for her recent behavior was marred by her emotional reaction — her love/hate conflict was all-consuming. Although Doreen did not at first see a connection between her nightmares and her lack of control over her own destiny, she agreed that there was probably a good possibility that her feelings of helplessness were a key precipitating factor. It was only after she had been enrolled in the drug-counselling program and began to take responsibility for her drug problem that the nightmares decreased in frequency and finally stopped.

Doreen then recounted a recent violent altercation between her and her mother. Doreen started to giggle about the incident.

It occurred after a football rally at school when Doreen returned home in a drunken stupor after having consumed a fifth of scotch over a two-hour time period. She attempted to ride her bicycle back home. Fortunately she was able to reach her home without accidental physical injury. However, her mother's greeting more than made up for lack of bodily harm. She started punching Doreen. Doreen did not remain passive. She punched back.

"She gave me a black eye — the cops came — I guess the neighbors heard us fighting and called them. I locked myself in the bathroom." Doreen's voice reached a fever pitch — she grinned from ear to ear. "I was afraid that I'd be arrested if I came out of the bathroom, so I stayed until they left. The cops are always comin' to break up our fights. They know us by now. They've come about ten times this year alone." Doreen chuckled. "My mom's boyfriend also fights with her. She has a boyfriend now and they don't really get along. He reminds me of my dad — always cursin' and free with his fists. The cops have been over to break up their fights too."

Doreen's mood suddenly shifted to serious. She said that she was afraid of her mother's boyfriend and didn't want to spend much time with her mother because of his violent outbursts.

Her major concern, however, was her own drinking problem and the possibility that she could somehow grow up to be like her mother — drug dependent, poor, violently angry and "crazy".

"It's not hard for me to sit down and drink," Doreen

continued. "After a while it goes down like water. Sometimes I mix pot with alcohol." Doreen took a long drag on her cigarette.

We continued to discuss her concerns about her future. Although she was relatively pleased with her control over substances and that she was able to remain drug free for over three months, she was hesitant about the possibility of long-term success. Her vision of herself was clouded over by strong and countless images of her violent alcoholic father and her violent alcoholic mother. They were overwhelming to her. There was a lack of stability in her life. Most of her childhood had been spent in the midst of chaos — moving from one location to another — from one foster home to another. She had been reared in an atmosphere of physical and emotional upheaval. All of the adult men in her life — her father, her mother's second husband and current boyfriend were violent. Alcoholism and violence dominated most of her childhood.

Doreen could not escape from the intense recollections of a childhood steeped in physical and mental anguish. She could not resurrect any untroubled memories. There were no remembrances of happy hugs, encouraging smiles or tender family discussions. There were no strong, but gentle men in her experience, there were no strong independent women in her life. She drew no comfort from her gnawing fear of becoming like her mother. Her future had no definition — Doreen could not verbalize her dreams about the future. She had no dreams, only major concerns. Prognosis for Doreeen would have to be guarded at this point. For Doreen, a support system does not exist. There was no interested teacher or adult friend of the family or involved grandparents or older sibling or concerned adult. Doreen's only hope for some chance to recover from her childhood victimization was the small positive success she was experiencing at the drug-counselling program. It was her only (though admittedly weak) link to recovery. In her mind addiction to substances and violent problem-solving were the norm. She had very little exposure, if any, to a drug-free, violence-free family situation.

There is very little reason to believe that under present circumstances, Doreen would be able to change her lifestyle, replete with maladaptive coping mechanisms. The most important factor was missing — encouragement. There was no person in her present life who cared enough to encourage her to set higher goals for herself. Doreen was utterly alone. As such, she had very little reason to thrive. She was on a suicide mission without a shred of hope for significant recovery.

I gazed into her 14-year-old face. Her eyes were cold and piercing. She sat cross-legged in a somewhat arrogant pose, furiously puffing one cigarette after another. On the surface she seemed mature and sure of herself. She had that *I can take care of myself attitude* about her. But underneath the surface, Doreen was a threatened unsure little girl, unready and unable to cope up with life's challenges. She had a simple compact ready-made solution in her alcohol and marijuana addiction. It was for Doreen a quick and easy escape from the intolerable memories of child- and wife-beating. Here was a human being without a family and without a reason for living. Her mother, father and grandparents were living, but they were spiritually and emotionally dead to Doreen. I wondered how this attractive young girl could survive her barren childhood. I doubted if she would ever be able to overcome such gargantuan obstacles on her own. There she sat a lost soul — a child without a future.

CHAPTER 8

Violence Begets Violence: A Mother's Perspective

QUESTION: Peggy, how did you meet your husband?

ANSWER: A blind date.

Q: What attracted you to him?

A: I can't think. When I first started going out with him, it was just something to do. I was very blunt about that. Well, if I don't have anything else better to do, I'll go out with you. He was marriage-minded. I was 18 and I was ready to leave home.

Q: Did he know that?

A: Yes.

Q: You confided in him?

A: He knew things weren't very good between my mother and me. She was the ruler of the house. She thrived on power and was very frustrated because of her own disappointments. So marriage seemed like a good way for me to get away from it all.

Q: How did your attitudes and ideas about your specific role in marriage affect the way you reacted to your husband's violence?

A: Violence for me was a way of life. When I was a kid, I was constantly being exposed to it. Violence in my marriage wasn't that much different. I had already learned to live with violence as a child. I knew that things would calm down after an outrage and life would go on as normal. But with my husband, I wasn't so sure that I'd be safe after one of his outbursts. He was a very big man and I believed that he could kill me if he had wanted to.

Q: Describe your mother.

A: She was 5'3" like me, very heavy. She was always throwing things at us. She'd bang my head into a wall every so often. That was when I felt like running away. There were times when I couldn't take gym in school because of the bumps and bruises. Sometimes she'd undress me and put me in a tub of hot water and then beat me with a coffee pot cord. Boy, did it sting! Because I felt so terribly rejected and unloved by my mother, I found myself always wanting to please her. I wanted to be liked by her and everyone else in my life. I had come to believe that I was really a bad person and that I deserved to be beaten. So, naturally, when my husband started beating me, I thought that if I showed him how much I loved him and did everything I could to please him, he'd love me back and I wouldn't get beaten.

Q: Did you ever run away from home because of your mother's beatings?

A: I thought about it, but after she calmed down, I lost the motivation to flee. She used to beat my sister too. But we were so confused about the whole thing. I knew that at times I needed to get away from mother, but I also wanted her to love me. I really felt bad for her — very sorry for her because I knew that she was sorry for beating us. It ripped me in half. The closest I came to running away was staying overnight at a friend's house. We used to confide in each other. Her parents were alcoholics and so we used to compare notes. She was never beaten, so I thought that she was better off than me.

Q: Did your father ever beat you as well?

A: My father was terribly subservient. When he was home and he felt that Mom had gone beyond the deep end, he would step in and they would fight. That's when I'd feel twice as guilty. I blamed myself for their fighting. My father, whom I dearly loved, held down two jobs to support the kids, but I think he wanted to stay away from home as much as possible. Sometimes Mom would get hysterical with him and throw things at him.

Q: How did your mother treat you when she wasn't lashing out at you?

A: She was very caring and supportive. This caused a lot of confusion in me. I didn't find out until this past summer that she had been abused by her mother as a child.

Q: Was your husband good to you when he wasn't abusive?

A: Yes, he was never abusive when he wasn't drunk. When he didn't have anything in him, he would never think of lifting a finger.

Q: Would you say that because he treated you well some of the times it made it hard for you to leave him?

A: Yes, and because I wanted to love and because I needed to be loved so badly.

Q: After your husband started beating you up, did you consider yourself battered?

A: No. I think it was a tragedy for me to be in my twenties and not even realize that violence was abnormal. I felt I was somehow responsible for it and I must be a rotten person. My self-image was terrible. It took me a long time to realize that I didn't cause him to beat me and that he beat me 'cause I just happened to be a convenient target for his rage.

Q: What made you change your attitude?

A: Just by observing my friends and how their husbands treated them. Most of them had good marriages. Their husbands didn't restrict them from going to school functions, or playing bingo — doing the ordinary things. I was basically confined to my home. I had to get permission to go anywhere. My friends weren't beaten. It made me start to question my marriage. I had to practically punch in at a time clock. He was insecure. He didn't trust me. He'd keep me in line by staying away from home for short periods of time. He would leave from work and come home in the wee hours of the morning. Or he'd stay away for a day or two. He always tried to make me feel responsible for driving him away. And I fell for his twisted logic.

I guess it all goes back to my childhood. My mother used to say that I was always ruining her day. I believed her. So when my husband accused me of messing up his life, I bought into it.

Q: What was your sexual relationship like?

A: I was subservient. He was extremely rough and I didn't have any previous sexual experience when we got married. I didn't like sex a whole lot. It wasn't after years that I got the nerve to tell him to stop being so aggressive. Intercourse was so disappointing that I really became extremely frustrated and tried hard not to be aroused. I contracted colitis, had a gastric stomach and a spastic colon, none of which I have anymore.

Q: Would he ever force himself?

A: Toward the very end of our marriage. At first I felt I had a wifely duty to cooperate. But as I began to stand up for myself, I started to withdraw from his advances. Sex became extremely difficult for me after the abuse I took during the day. I was devious about turning him down and used to insult him.

Q: How do you feel about sex now that you are no longer married to this man?

A: I have a healthier attitude as far as sex goes. I can enjoy it, but I really value a relationship based on friendship first.

For a good eight months after the divorce, I isolated myself from male companionship. I preferred female friends. I felt more relaxed with them. I couldn't get serious with any man during that period.

Q: Did you ever seek professional help?

A: Yes, my family doctor made me feel that my feelings were normal and that it was only a matter of time before I would trust men again. He was right.

Q: Did your ex-husband ever remarry?

A: Yes, and he beats his second wife. She reminds me of myself not too long ago. But she's in worse shape than I ever was. He beat her while they were dating. She knew what to expect and yet she married him. As far as I'm concerned, she walked in this situation with her eyes open. I have little sympathy for her.

Q: Is there a man in your life now?

A: Yes, I had gone out with him seven months before we became sexually intimate. We got married a few months ago.

Q: How does he treat you?

A: This is his second marriage. He felt that his ex-wife neglected him. We found in each other things that were missing in our lives. I'm the opposite of her and he's the opposite of my ex-husband.

Q: What kind of work does he do?

A: He's an open-road truck driver.

Q: How do you feel about other women who get battered by their husbands?

A: I feel empathy. But I get impatient with them. I can't help feeling, "If this is happening to you, you're allowing it. He's doing nothing to you that you're not letting him get away with. If you don't put up with it, he can't beat you."

Q: What advice would you give to other battered women?

A: I want them to understand that if they don't do something about their situation, I don't want to hear them bellyache about it. I really have a hard-nosed attitude that a woman better start learning to accept a certain amount of reality. And she needs a good solid dose of, "Hey! There's nobody else that has enough power to control your life. If he hits you, it's because you gave the control to him. If you don't like it, you do something about it. He's not going to change."

Q: Did women offer you any assistance or support when you were being battered?

A: Many over-sympathized and didn't give me a dose of reality. They weren't honest or tough enough. They'd say, "Why don't you get out of there?" But they wouldn't go the next step and help me make the plans or find another place. Or they'd say dumb things like, "You must like the beatings, that's why you stay." I needed women to help me see the steps that needed to be taken to get out. Nobody really offered me practical help.

Q: Did you and your ex-husband have any children?

A: Yes, two boys and a girl.

Q: Do you have any special problems with them?

A: Yes, after I left my husband, I began to lash out at the kids with screaming fits of rage. I guess all of the anger and frustration from an abusive childhood and an abusive marriage began to emerge when I had the freedom to express it.

Q: Did you ever beat the children?
A: I never touched them. But I threatened them. This did a lot of damage to them. I'd get up on top of them and scream. It's a wonder they didn't have — nervous breakdowns. When I look back and think how crazy I acted, I feel terrible.

Q: Did they ever see you get beaten by your ex-husband?

Q: Yes, all the time, even when they were babies. They'd get hysterical and scream and yell. They'd hide their heads and cover their ears. If they tried to run out of the room, my "ex" would force them to come back in and watch. He'd say, "I want you to see how stupid your mother is."

Q: Did any of your children ever try to stop him from beating you?

A: No. They were too frightened. He'd beat them. He never injured them. My daughter was five and my oldest boy was eight when I left him. They were very tense all the time. They'd give me advice like, "Don't do that, Mom, or Dad will get upset," or "Mom, don't say that 'cause Dad will get mad." They were constantly trying to make peace. What a burden it must have been for them!

Q: How did you get along with your sons?

A: I was very hard on my youngest boy. He reminded me of my husband. We got off to a lousy start even before he was born. I didn't want him all through the pregnancy. After he was born, I was very sick and had to stay in the hospital for two months. He was confined to the nursery right after his birth. I was too sick to hold him. When I got home, I was still sick. I was down to 89 pounds. I couldn't take care of him or my other boy. Mom and Dad tried helping out. They took us all down to their place. I finally got back on my feet.

Q: What were the circumstances that prompted your leaving?

A: I came home from the hospital after he had cracked my ribs.

That very night — my first night home, he started fighting again! He's a big man. The hospital social worker had tried to discourage me from going back home. But I didn't listen. She warned me, "One day you'll realize that people don't have story book love and that you're not going to live happily ever after."

That night I was rushed back to the hospital because of a terrible beating. That's when I decided to leave him. When I recovered, I took the first opportunity to leave. I put some clothes in a green garbage bag, wrapped the kids in blankets, got into the car and drove off. I didn't have more than five dollars in my pocket at the time.

Q: Did you know where you were going?

A: No, I just drove. I cried. I shook. I was scared.

Q: What about the children?

A: They were scared to death.

Q: What kind of physical condition were you in after you left your husband?

A: I was in terrible shape. I couldn't cope. I had an emotional shutdown. I got to the point where I couldn't even get out of bed. The children were on their own. Somebody must have been watching over them.

Q: What happened?

A: When I decided to leave home, I took the children. We lived in our station wagon for about two months. It was hell. I took them to school from the car. They used to beg me to go back home, but I didn't give in. My sister took us in for another three months until I had enough money for a deposit on an apartment.

Q: What was your husband's reaction to your leaving?

A: He harassed me and the kids for a five-year period. He came after us with a gun and threatened my sister or any friends who took us in. One winter I was walking down the street to the supermarket with my daughter and a friend. He spotted us and pulled up to the curb in his van. Then he ordered me to "get in". When I didn't, he tried to run me down, but I jumped out of the way and ducked into a laundromat.

Q: What else did he do to try to get you back?

A: He assaulted me in the apartment because I had tried to have him arrested for reckless endangering. After New Years he started harassing me over the phone. He threatened me all hours of the day and night. He promised to kill me if I went to court. One afternoon at about two o'clock, he phoned to say that he was coming to kill me. I called my lawyer who gave me the number of a battered women's shelter. I was hanging by a thread.

Q: Did you go to the shelter?

A: They took us in and I was free to follow through with court action without fear. The kids were brought into court. He pleaded guilty to a class B misdemeanor. He got a three-month prison term which was suspended for one year on probation, plus a fine. During that year on probation he remarried.

Q: What kind of visitation schedule did you work out with the court?

A: I got full custody of the kids and my "ex" was allowed to visit them. We worked out a schedule, but he never stuck to it. Sometimes he wouldn't visit for months. My middle son didn't want to see him for the first four months after the divorce. He had a lot of anger and resentment.

Q: Did you ever find yourself regretting moving out?

A: No, never. It was murder, but I didn't want to go back to the violence. I didn't know where the next dime was coming from. We were very poor. I had to make the children learn that there was more to life than just material things. One Christmas, my oldest son asked, "Is Mrs. Santa gonna be poor this year?" But my middle boy jumped in, "We've got what a lot of other people don't have. We have each other." I never doubted the wisdom of moving out again.

Q: Did you have any serious behavior problems with any of the children?

A: My middle boy gave me the most trouble. He's had to have lots of psychiatric help. As a youngster he was always physical and had trouble interacting with other kids. When he was two and a half, he'd mess his diaper on an average of three to five times a day. He'd go into his room or sit in the closet and remove the diaper and then go through the room with the mess. Next he'd sit near the toy box and smear every single toy, the door knobs, the bed, walls, windows and sheets with excrement. This went on for three or four times a day.

Q: Go on.

A: When he was three he'd come up to me when I was doing dishes and pull himself up on my legs and gouge his nails into my legs until they bled.

Q: How did you react?

A: I found myself rejecting him. That's when I went to the mental hygiene clinic.

A: Was that helpful?

A: Not really. They thought nothing was wrong. They said he'd "outgrow it". So I discontinued counselling.

Q: Did he improve on his own?

A: No. When he was in first grade the principal called to say that they were expelling him because he had tried to hang a cat with a coat hanger! I was relieved by this. Finally someone felt that his behavior wasn't normal. His teacher suggested intensive therapy even residential treatment.

Q: Was he ever a threat to anyone at home?

A: At one time he sat on his sister until her face turned blue. I caught him choking her to death. If I hadn't stopped him, my daughter might be dead today.

Q: What did you decide to do?

A: I placed him in a residential treatment facility where he lived for three years. It was fantastic. It was one of the hardest decisions of my life, but it was the right thing to do. He came out of there a better boy.

Q: How often did you see him while he was away?

A: At first I saw him for one hour, then two hours until I worked up to eight hours per week which was their maximum. After the staff felt both he and I were ready, they allowed him to come home on weekends. The summer before his last year they arranged for him to sleep at home while he went to day school with counselling sessions after school.

Q: How did he adjust to a residential setting?

A: He thought I was getting rid of him. I felt guilty in the beginning. It was painful taking his suitcase full of clothes and dropping him off with complete strangers. He seemed angry and hurt. If people only knew how many times I would go and sit in a church and cry! But I had to do what was best for him at the time.

Q: How is he now?

A: He's the best adjusted of all three kids. He doesn't even hide the fact that he had to go into residential treatment. He's comfortable talking about it.

Q: Where did you find the strength to face up to all your problems and to do something about them?

A: Through praying. I think that a lot of good things couldn't have happened if it hadn't been for the grace of God. To me, God is a great source of love and if nothing else, I know I am loved spiritually. I need to believe that there's somebody greater than me helping to carry me. "Let go and let God," is my motto. Prayer gave me the courage to do what I needed to do — take me and the kids out of a crazy home and start a new life.

Q: What are your hopes for the future?

A: Looking back, I'd say that I don't really know how I survived all the abuse and the misery that began with my mother's beatings. I can only hope and pray that my children will not suffer as much in their adult lives as I have. Though they have been exposed to a lot of pain, they have seen me struggle against it.

I pray that my daughter walks away from this experience with strength of character and that my sons will not act like their father did when they have their own families. I hope

that I have given them the example they need to live normal
peaceful lives. It will be my reward. To know that my
decisions will stop the violence for the next generation
makes the pain less intense.

CHAPTER 9

The Unexpected Victim

I met Angela about 17 years ago. She was a regular visitor of the park on Riverside Drive not far from the main campus of Columbia University. Young mothers, nannys, grand-moms and babysitters would congregate daily around the sandbox, socializing with each other while the children played in the park. Everyone looked forward to days when the weather was good. It was always nice to break up the day's routine with a visit to the park. Most of us felt that the children who were too young for nursery school would benefit from interaction with their peers. We discussed this quite openly. There was, however, another good derived from such social experiences. While the children were learning to socialize with each other, the grown-ups were enjoying each other's company. We were regulars at the sandbox. Day after day we met in the park. We learned a lot from each other, but we also learned quite a bit about each other. Some of us struck up lasting friendships.

Angela and I became very close. She was middle-aged, in her early forties and physically very attractive. She was a sculptor by training, but did not earn her living from this.

Her husband was a tenured professor at one of the law schools in the New York metropolitan area, so it seemed quite odd at the time that Angela needed to babysit. She was always impeccably dressed and well-spoken, very sensitive and quite interesting. I wondered why a university professor's wife with a bachelor's degree in the fine arts and two teenage children of her own would find it necessary to baby-sit for other people's children. Somehow it did not add up.

Then one day late in the afternoon when all of the other women and their children had left the park for their apartments, Angela asked me if she could stop over at my place for a short time. She wanted to talk to me about something personal that was bothering her, and she didn't want to take the chance of being interrupted by a latecomer who might come by the sandbox with a child. I sensed urgency in her voice so naturally invited her up. It was then over freshly brewed cups of coffee in the kitchen of my Columbia University owned apartment that I began to fit together the pieces of the puzzle.

Angela began to quake. I was alarmed by her lack of composure. It was not like her to become "unglued". Naturally, I was concerned. Angela was always so self-possessed, so sure of herself. I thought that she might be seriously ill or that one of her children was in poor health; maybe her husband had been fired from his job. I was wrong about all three suppositions. Angela started to unravel the details.

She began with her ordeal of the previous evening. Her problem centered around her husband's behavior. She could hardly get the words out. She was trying to find the words. She said that he had started drinking early in the afternoon. He would usually finish teaching his last class on Thursdays at 1:45 p.m., then stay on campus for student conferences or research in the library, but he had cancelled his appointments for the afternoon because of some "personal" problem.

Angela said that for the past six months her husband had been involved with a young student of his. Yesterday she broke off their relationship without warning. This was not his first affair. He had been unfaithful ever since the birth of their last child.

Angela had lost count of his many love interests. She had decided a long time ago that she would not give him up. She liked being a professor's wife, but more importantly, she could not visualize herself alone and divorced. She explained that her Catholic upbringing offered no solution other than endurance and prayer as a way of coping with her unfortunate circumstances. Infidelity was, of course, a great source of pain for Angela. She was prepared to bear the humiliation of one affair after another and to accept the degradation of one drink too many.

She was, however, not ready for the fits of rage and verbal abuse which almost always accompanied his drinking bouts. One such episode had occurred the night before. He was devastated by the shock of his ruptured love affair. Angela explained that his abusive behavior had become more physical in recent years. She speculated that the combination of drink and "mid-life crisis" were in high gear at the present time and that these two factors were leading him to act out violently.

Last night's incident was more traumatic than usual. Angela began to divulge the details of the evening's events. She noted that what had happened was so horrendous as to cause her to reach a turning point in her life. She had made up her mind. Her life had reached its lowest ebb and she wanted to do something constructive that would benefit both her and her children. I asked her what had happened.

She paused and then blurted out in a restrained whisper that about 6:30 p.m., after she and the children had finished their supper, her busband had entered the kitchen and demanded dinner. He had locked himself in the bedroom ever since returning home from the university — Angela assumed that he would probably sleep this one off like so many others, therefore, she and the children did not expect him to join them for dinner. Surprisingly, he had emerged from the bedroom a "raging maniac". "What's for dinner?" he boomed. Angela continued, "One thing led to another and before you knew it, he was swearing all over the place, screaming at me and at the kids. I couldn't help myself. Usually I keep quiet when he gets crazy, but last night I got sucked into the argument. That's where I made my big mistake. He got louder and louder and I got bolder and bolder. One thing led to another and before you knew it, he was brandishing a chef's knife that I keep in one of those knife holders on the kitchen counter. The children were still in the kitchen during all the squabbling. When they saw the knife being waved like a sword, they both started to scream and run for the door. I followed them shouting four-letter insults at him. He yelled, 'I'm going to cut you all into tiny little pieces and then throw you in the gutter.' We weren't going to take any chances.

"He was always nasty with drink in him, but last night he had murder on his mind. The children and I ran outside the apartment house and into the street and then over to Broadway where I found a phone booth and dialed 911. I couldn't go back to the apartment without a police escort. I'll never forget my kids' faces. They were really scared. I must have looked scared too. I remember that my hands were shaking so much I couldn't fit my finger in the telephone dial at first."

I sat there in a state of shock never dreaming that these things could happen to such a fine family. I grew up thinking that educated middle class families were immune to such behavior. I was puzzled, confused. It wasn't that I doubted Angela. She had never ever given me reason to question her veracity. She was not prone to hyperbole. I believed her, but I could not understand why a respectable university professor would chase after his wife and children with a knife! I thought, "What would make a person in his circumstances act like a menacing beast?" I immediately felt compassion for Angela and her children.

"What happened after you called the police," I asked.

"They came about a half hour later. My kids and I sat in the park across the street until we saw the squad car parked outside our building. We approached the police as they started to enter the foyer. I told them to take him out of the apartment because he would probably kill us. They

followed me to the half-opened door which I pushed in
with my hand. The two officers walked past me and began
to search the apartment for my husband. I stayed in the hall
of the building near the stairs with the children — just in
case there'd be more trouble. I fantasized that there would
be a wild gun chase, gunshots, and that I might even be
taken hostage by my husband if he were desperate enough.
My imagination was running wild. I worked myself into a
sweat. I felt that anything could happen and that somebody
was going to get killed — either me or the kids or all of us.

"After what seemed to be an eternity, the police came out
of the apartment alone. I had expected to witness an ugly
confrontation between them and my husband. When I
didn't, I came out from behind the stairwell and confidently
approached the responding officers. 'What happened? I
asked. Isn't my husband inside? Why isn't he with you?' They
explained that he was indeed inside but that he apparently
had passed out on the kitchen floor. The police picked him
up and dropped him into our bed. They felt that he would
sleep it off and would probably be of no further threat to us.
They said that we'd be safe and not to worry.

"Their advice, of course, did not calm me to any great
extent. I was relieved that he was no longer conscious, but
I didn't trust the situation. I instructed the children to tiptoe
into the apartment and to speak only in whispers so as not
to disturb their sleeping father. The last thing I wanted was
for him to wake up and start where he left off. We crept into
our apartment like thieves in the night. We had no choice.
As much as a part of me wanted to leave the apartment,
another practical part encouraged me to stay. Where could I
go? Both my parents were dead. I don't have any brothers or
sisters. I was too embarrassed to call you, thinking I'd be an
imposition. So we wound up staying at home under most
distressing conditions. We stayed together in the living
room. Eventually the children fell asleep, but I managed to
hold vigil the entire evening. By six a.m. I stirred the
children out of their temporary beds and instructed them to
get dressed quietly and hurriedly. My plan was to be out of
the house before my husband would awaken. They took

their school books and we headed for Broadway. It was the hardest morning of my life. Luckily I was able to get hold of my senses during the night. I thought about what my life was like and what I had become over the years.

"For the first time I was able to see things from a different perspective. All the years that I had spent covering up his behavior, denying how really devastated I felt, and hoping that he'd mend his ways and we'd go off into the sunset became crystal clear for me. In the quiet of the night I was able to distinguish between my fantasies and harsh reality. It hit me right between the eyes. My marriage was both a joke and a tragedy. I took a hard look at the children sleeping on the floor and broke down into uncontrollable sobs. I remembered the look of fear and shock on their faces during the crazed chase just a few hours before and I felt disgustingly guilty about having exposed them to such jeopardy. 'This will never happened again,' I vowed."

Angela broke down at this heightened sense of aware-ness. She realized what the ramifications of her vow would mean. Her love for her children was primary. They would be the catalysts for her turning point. If she were to decide her destiny without the children in the equation, she surely would have chosen to stay with her husband, to give him another chance to mend his ways and prove his love for her. But she was not about to gamble with the children. She wanted to protect them from any future threats to life and limb. And so she was prepared to do whatever was necessary to keep the vow. I asked her what she was thinking of doing and she answered that she would have to leave him for good.

"Oh, God!" she exclaimed, "I don't want to do it, but I know I have to. I'm really scared. I have no income and haven't held a full-time job in 20 years. But I can't expect the children to be martyrs because I behave like one. I'm going down to Legal Aid on Monday and see what I can do about a separation or divorce. If I can get him out of the house, at least the children and I would have a roof over our heads. That's where I plan to start. But I need a place for us to stay over the weekend. I have a supply of checks and a charge card so I don't need any money. I just need a place. Do you think that I could stay here with the children until it's safe to return home?"

Angela's sense of logic impressed me at this point. She seemed to be thinking very clearly and had proposed a methodical plan of extrication. I wanted to help her out of her predicament and so I assured her that she could stay until she could safely return to her apartment. She thanked me with a full sigh of relief and said that she would have to take the subway and meet her children on the steps of the Public Library on 42nd Street. She had instructed them to go there after school and to wait until she could meet them. Angela grabbed her shoulder bag and "flew" out of the door. She was determined to make things right for her children.

Angela stayed the weekend plus 10 more days. There were too many loose ends to pick up with court orders and legal action. The female attorney at the Legal Aid office had intimidated her at first. She urged Angela to leave her husband, her possessions and her home and to find a full-time job for self-support. She felt that Angela's husband was a poor risk. Her experience told her that men with histories of drinking problems and violent behavior could not be relied upon for alimony and/or child support and that she should be practical about her options.

Angela felt that she, the victim, was being asked to pay the steepest penalties — to break up home and run the risk of being poverty stricken. She felt resentment. She felt cheated and robbed. After all, wasn't it her husband who had committed adultery numerous times and wasn't it her husband who had acted irrationally and menacingly? Wasn't it he who had tried to kill her and their children with a chef's knife? Why, then, was she being asked to pay the price? Why was she being treated like the guilty party and why was her husband allowed to resume his lifestyle without pain or sacrifice? Angela muddled over these objections. She tried hard not to become bitter, but she could not wrest herself from her strong feelings about justice and retribution. Angela, therefore, rejected the advice of the experienced attorney. Her idealism prevailed and she was determined to fight every inch of the way through the courts.

Angela's husband left their apartment and moved in with a former girlfriend. Angela continued to babysit to help pay for food and incidentals, but she could not bring herself to search for a more lucrative full-time job in the world of business and industry. She was a sculptor at heart. She wanted to be able to pursue a career as a freelance painter — to break into the art world and exhibit her paintings in various shows from time to time. She had started babysitting approximately five years ago when it became apparent to her that her husband would not pay for her art supplies without complaining and arguing. Babysitting gave her enough freedom to paint part of the day. She was grateful for whatever hours she could get during the daytime.

But things were different now that her husband had moved out. Angela found herself in a perpetual financial crisis. She was beginning to regret her decision to separate from her husband. Maybe she had been too hasty. Maybe she should have forgiven him and tried harder for a reconciliation. She and the children seemed to be the ones who were suffering the most. Her husband was now extremely comfortable in the arms of someone else. He still had his university paycheck. He was not in any way being inconvenienced by the separation. Angela resented what she viewed as an unjust outcome. After all, she wasn't the one who had committed adultery nor was she an alcoholic with an uncontrollable temper.

After several months of court battles for alimony and child support, Angela was weary but not discouraged. She felt that all she needed to do was persist and eventually things would work out in her favor. I saw her agonize over her husband's "lack of conscience", her phrase of choice. He was never on time with the rent and with the children's tuition. Medical bills and gas and electric were in arrears. She hadn't sculpted in months. She could no longer afford art supplies. Besides, running back and forth to court was beginning to wear her out both emotionally and physically. In spite of the hardships, Angela refused to look for a better paying job on principle. She was determined to fight this out to the finish.

I watched Angela as she struggled to survive. It was taking its toll on her. More noticeably, it was seriously affecting her children. The constant turmoil in the home over financial problems — Angela's overt unhappiness with her circumstances, her growing bitterness and discontent with life and her disillusionment with the justice system were creating an unstable home life for the children. Their grades were dropping and they no longer seemed interested in friends and school activities. Her son was becomming a recluse. After school and on weekends he would confine himself to his room or watch TV. Her daughter was also spending a good deal of her free time in the home. This was unusual for them. They always had had lots of friends and were usually busy with one thing or another at school or in the neighborhood. The difference in their behavior was very dramatic.

At first, they were angry with their father for all of his aberrations. They loathed his drinking and his fits of violence. They despised his adulterous affairs. They were upset with his irresponsible neglect of their physical well-being. While Angela was waging war in the courts, internal battles were being fought by the children. They did not have the forum of the courtroom or the lawyer's office to release their discontent. As time passed, their anger turned away from their absentee father and towards their mother. She, somehow in their mind, had become the villain. Why couldn't their mother give up her quest, accept the world as it was and make a new life for herself? They were tired of the interruptions in their lives. They were frustrated with their father's delinquent support payments. They secretly wished for a time when their mother would compromise her principles to some extent. Why couldn't she work and petition the courts for child support?

Angela refused to compromise her principles. She fought her disturbing battle for the next seven years. During that period her son attempted suicide twice, and her daughter tried it once. While they grew indifferent towards their distant father, intense feelings of anger for their mother continued to build. She was the object of most of their

negative feelings. By the time the children had finished
college, Angela has lost their love and respect. They were
not interested in her private crusade. They were children
with simple but essential needs. They needed a stable
parent in the home who would provide for them and offer
them encouragement and emotional support. Angela,
herself, was a very needy person. She was exhausted most of
the time, battle fatigued and resentful. She was in no
condition to give the children what they required. The
children did not understand her agony.

When their father left after that horrible frenzied chase
through the house with the chef's knife, the children were
relieved. They agreed with their mother's decision to
separate from him. He had been a constant source of pain
for them and their mother. They imagined that their lives
would improve after his departure. Their expectations and
hopes, however, were dashed by the second set of problems
facing them and their mother. These problems helped pale
their memories of drinking binges and loud profanities and
overturned furniture and shouted threats to life and limb.
While they despised the past with their father as chief brute,
they heaped their intense feelings of fury upon their mother
because she was physically present and because she never
completely cut the cord of dependence to him. What they as
children wanted most was a fresh start — a second chance
to live their lives in quiet secure surroundings. They
couldn't grow with constant reminders of their father's
infidelity and negligence. Their mother's lingering bitterness with their father and the family courts did not
extinguish their profound sense of loss and abandonment.
They felt deserted by society, by their father and by their
mother. It did not occur to them that if their mother had
stayed with their father, they could have eventually been
physically harmed. While this may have been a probable
consequence of remaining with their father, it became less
important in their eyes after the separation.

During their long ordeal the children could not see the
light at the end of the tunnel. Their father's indifference kept
reinforcing their feelings of despair. Things never seemed to

improve for them. Month after month, year after year it was the same. It was a lesson in futility for them. People who attempt suicide usually do not believe that things can improve and that with time comes change. One of the reasons why teenagers commit suicide is because they do not grasp this possibility. Angela's children were caught in a web of unending turmoil. Seven continuous years of fighting and struggling against all odds made it impossible for them to visualize a positive resolution to their problems. Suicide appealed to them because it offered a way out of their painful dilemma.

Angela's decision to physically separate herself from her violent alcoholic husband was sound. She did so to insure her safety and that of her children. That her husband's behavior was irresponsible and threatening is indisputable. That she chose not to completly sever the ties to him was regrettable. That the children were traumatized pre- and post-separation is tragic. In cases such as this one, the best interest of the children should prevail. Recognizing the enormous inequities in the judicial system, which are still now being addressed, Angela's long-term war against that system prevented her from establishing herself as an independent woman of means. Cutting the cord would have meant financial hardship for Angela and her children. No one is debating this. Her background and professional experience would not have led to a high-paying job in the work force. She would have been forced to abandon her lifestyle to several notches below her current status. Given the alternatives as unjust as they were, a more stable, albeit hard, home life for her and her children could have occurred had she not devoted all of her energies towards the attainment of spousal support. An equal pursuit of personal improvement goals through employment counsel-ling and additional educational training could possibly have enabled Angela to achieve personal satisfaction as well as a better paying job and would have lessened the tensions and frustrations of everyday family living.

CHAPTER 10

Renewal

Paula married Richard Freed, her college sweetheart, soon after college graduation. Not much thought had been given to it. They married because their friends were doing it and because both of them had lived together for a six-month period during their last semester at school.

Paula's parents were never abusive to each other or to her — her childhood and adolescence were not marred by violent upheaval. So when Rich's drinking binges shortly after their marriage resulted in violent attacks on her, she "went into shock."

Her steps toward survival paved her life and their marriage. At first Paula withdrew both sexually and emotionally. Later, when Rich's behavior began to endanger the physical well-being of their little girl, Paula decided with the help of an attorney to seek refuge at a women's shelter. This decision caused Rich to take a long hard look at himself. Consequently, he sought help for his drinking problem, which has brought about a reconciliation.

Paula confided that moving out to a shelter gave both of them an opportunity to look at themselves and to examine their relationship apart from each other. She discovered that she didn't have to put up with the violence, and he learned that he would have to quit drinking if he wanted his wife and child back.

Paula's leaving forced Rich to put things into perspective and to evaluate his behavior. It also made him realize that if he didn't change, he would have to face a possible divorce. He chose to work on the former. They have both since celebrated the birth of their second child — a symbol of their renewed love for each other.

We're back together again — Rich and I. Everything's better now. He's joined AA — it was his decision — he made it on his own without any help from me. It's been just two years now since we almost broke up and I really feel confident that we're going to make it. I'm a member of Al-Anon — the meetings really do help a lot. Some of the other women are in worse shape than I ever was, and they're coping. This gives me hope. If they can do it, so can I.

I guess when I look back on everything that's happened — all the ugly incidents, I find it hard to believe that I was the woman it happened to. What I was then and what I am today bears very little resemblance. That woman in my painful memories is a shadow and I don't identify with her any more.

My feet are firmly planted on the ground now. That's saying a lot for me. It means I have matured, have grown up and that I feel I can determine my own future. It means I'm healthy. I used to be very "sick" in my thinking and my actions. I was one of those romantic weaklings. Romance was always on my mind and what was really unhealthy was my insane expecta-tion that fairy tale endings — happy endings are readily available to all true believers. I know better now. And you know something, the more I think of it, the more I know that belief in fairy tale endings is the opiate of the victim. I mean if you're in a bad situation, and you do nothing to change the circumstances, because you're waiting for someone else to make the first move or because you expect a miracle to happen, or a hero on a white horse to whisk you away, then you condition yourself into accepting your lot in life. You think of yourself as a hostage who needs someone else to rescue you. You wait and you wait until it happens. You keep telling yourself that something outside yourself — like the U.S. Cavalry — will ride in out of a cloud of dust and you will be saved. When I think of how I conned myself during those four years of abuse, I begin to feel a rage come over me. I don't like to dwell on those images for too long. They're negative and they don't add to the quality of my life today. But they're good to click on and off every now and then when I think I'm going to fall into the romantic trap of settling any problems that Rich and I may have to solve in our marriage.

You know, when I married him about six years ago, even though we had been living together for six months prior to the marriage, I never suspected that he had a violent streak. We were very much in love — college sweethearts. All our friends were getting married after graduation and so naturally, we followed suit. Since then we've both got graduate degrees in teaching. We should have got degrees in personal communication.

My childhood was very quiet. Mom and Dad never battled. Oh, yes, they disagreed about things — Dad was headstrong — but never abusive. So when Rich started to get nasty with me, I went into shock. I was confused and the only thing I could think of was to hang on to my dreams of being rescued.

Rich used to drink when we were in college — so did everybody else. He continued to drink after we married. I didn't see anything wrong with it. That it could be a sign of trouble never entered my mind. During the early months of our marriage we had fights — mostly because I turned off. As you would guess, this made matters worse. He drank more to escape my rejection. We'd argue about how I wasn't fulfilling my role as wife. But none of his beatings or guilt trips changed my decision to withdraw sexually from him. I preferred it that way. You could say that it was a form of protest. In fact, as I think back, I withdrew in every other way and focused all my attention on our infant daughter.

But things didn't work out. His drinking didn't stop. He couldn't think straight. I made the mistake of assuming that I

could reason with an alcoholic — I expected him to change
while I made myself available as his whipping post. I suppose
I wasn't operating with a full deck either. Imagine, I thought
that I could make him stop drinking by rejecting his sexual
advances and still live under the same roof with him. Any fool
could have seen the repercussions of such an arrangement.
What I was doing was giving him a double message. "I'll stick
around for you to break my bones, and then I'll ignore you
after you do it because then you'll understand what you've
done and mend your ways." Aside from being irrational, that
thinking was suicidal. It could have been homicidal, too!

I'm thinking back to the time of my first pregnancy. I find
it hard to go back. We didn't plan to have a child. I think the
prospect of added responsibility made Rich nervous. Needless
to say, the beatings increased. Here I was, at my most
vulnerable moment, pregnant and my husband declared war
on me and our unborn child. One minute he wanted the
child, the next minute he was swearing and punching me in
the abdomen. When he was drinking, he cursed the baby.
When he was sober, he'd go on and on about how happy he
was about becoming a father. I think that the pregnancy put an
extra strain on things 'cause I had to quit my job and we had
just purchased a home.

Surprisingly, after our daughter, Tia, was born, he tried to
control his drinking on his own. The birth actually had a
sobering effect on him. Unfortunately, it didn't last very long.

One night in a drunken rage, he put a lamp through the
wall. The noise of the crash awakened Tia. She got out of her
crib and followed Rich into our bedroom. He jumped onto
the bed and she crawled up next to him. He was so stoned, he
started beating her. There was a lot of remorse on his part
afterwards. But I was too stunned to care about his remorse.
My daughter's life was more important to me. By morning I
had taken a good hard look at myself and decided to contact
a lawyer.

"What can I do?" I asked my attorney. "I don't want a
divorce; I just want him out of the house."

For the first time since we were married, I became aware of
my options. Since my husband was an alcoholic, I was advised

to get out of the house before the legal papers arrived. Next I was given the number of a local shelter which I promptly called.

It was a good plan. Rich had changed jobs that year, so he was out that night. I packed everything up, took the baby and the car and left. I brought clothes, my checkbook, charge cards — a friend took the dog. The last thing I did was to tack a note with a magnet on the refrigerator door. The note read, "If you want to know where I am, contact my attorney", and I left him the name and number if he would want to get in touch. He did call the attorney who was sensitive enough not to reveal the location of the shelter. But he did reassure Rich that Tia and I were safe — not to worry and that we'd keep in touch through the attorney. Something must have clicked at that point because Rich didn't waste any time going to AA and then getting himself a lawyer.

We went to court a week later. The court ruling was very clear. Rich had three days to leave. And he left without incident. He left the house spotless. I was amazed. There was probably a lot of guilt. I didn't know what to think. I had expected him to become vindictive. Instead, he became more cooperative.

I stayed in the shelter for about three weeks while Rich was ordered by the court to make the mortgage payments on our home. I decided to return home and face a whole new set of problems centering around communication. We were like two strangers trying to get acquainted for the first time. Visitation was left open and sometimes he'd drop over everyday. It varied though. The judge ruled that he could visit as long as I felt comfortable and that if I had wanted a set rule, it could be once a week. I kept it flexible since Rich was very pleasant during visits. But I didn't allow him to take Tia away from the house. He was to visit her at home in my presence — that was the condition.

I think that getting out when I did saved our marriage. Taking Tia away for a while jolted him into changing. He knew I wasn't going to let him harm our daughter. He's even admitted that what I did made him take a hard look at himself and that he didn't like what he saw.

CHAPTER 11

What Can I Do?

How the Battered Wife Can Get Help

If I am a battered wife, I can help myself by asking myself the questions,

> "Do I want to remain with my husband?"
> "Is my marriage worth saving?"
> "Does my husband feel as strongly as I do about saving the marriage and is he willing to do whatever is necessary to work with me to change the situation?"
> "Do I have a support system?"
> "Are there family and friends nearby?"
> "If I have ever left my husband, what was his reaction? Remorseful, regretful, apologetic?"

If the answers to the above questions are *yes*, then the course of action for the battered wife who chooses to stay is as follows:

a. Talk over your goals with your husband. Encourage him to obtain counselling or therapy or to join a men's support group.

b. Discuss your problem with a close and trusted family member or friend. Get your feelings out into the open. Don't deny what's happening. Be honest and take a long hard look at yourself and your marriage. Make a pact with a friend or family member for shelter if an emergency should occur.

c. Contact your local battered women's shelter and become a member of a support group. Become familiar with other community resources and legal alternatives. Consult with a lawyer or a legal services representative.

d. If you have a job, don't quit it when you tend to get depressed about your situation. Stay in the mainstream. Isolation can lead to more serious depression and may even distort your perception about finding a way out of your dilemma.

e. If you are unemployed, think seriously about finding a job or about seeking job training. If things worsen, you will be better equipped to extricate yourself from the situation because you will have a means of financial support. Prepare for the worst — save money, find a job, get job-training, be as financially independent as is possible.

f. Develop outside interests and get involved in the community. This will help overcome feelings of isolation, low self-esteem and helplessness.

g. Be aware of triggering situations that from experience you know will lead to violence. Resolve to leave the house before the arguing reaches the physical level. Remove yourself from the house — drive to a relative, go to the mall. You can't be beaten if you're not present. Call home before returning. Talk to your husband first. Determine if he's calmed down and if it's safe to return. Stay with a friend or relative if it's not.

h. Seek counselling for your children to help them to cope with the stresses and emotional drain of living in a dangerous environment. Talk to the children about their feelings. Let them know that you will do everything you can to protect them and that they should be ready to leave the house with you if there is a threat of physical harm.

i. Consider family counselling or marriage counselling so that an objective third party can help you to find better ways of coping with stress and conflict.

j. Find out how you and your husband can alleviate stress in your lives. Check out resources in your area. Many people are experiencing positive results with the help of biological-feedback machines, meditation, Yoga, encounter groups. Finding serenity, meaning and focus are important goals. Holistic health centers and chiropractors are good sources of information and possible referrals.

If I am a battered wife but I am not sure if I should leave, I should ask myself the following questions:

"Has the violence persisted for a long period of time — years?"

"Do the episodes occur very frequently — once a month or every week?"

"Even if the violence doesn't occur all that frequently, is the level of violence severe?"

"Have I ever been hospitalized with serious injuries?"

"Have the children ever been physically hurt?"

"Are the children showing signs of emotional stress?"

"Are the children doing poorly in school?"

"Do they seem withdrawn?"

"Do they neglect to invite other children over to play?"

"Are any of them bullies in the school yard?"

"Are any of the older children missing school, getting failing grades, talking about dropping out of school, drinking or taking drugs?"

"Have any of the children run away at any time?"

"Have any of the children attempted suicide at any time?"

"Have any of the children tried to intervene in a fight between me and my husband, and were they ever physically harmed while trying to protect me from my husband's rage?"

"Do I feel trapped and am I getting more and more

depressed with time?"

"Am I avoiding friends and family?"

"Am I taking tranquilizers or turning to alcohol or food for comfort?"

"Do I wish that I were dead?"

"Do I ever feel like killing my husband?"

"Is my husband an alcoholic or drug abuser?"

"Do I feel that he needs help to conquer his addictions before he can begin to change his violent behavior?"

"Am I reasonably convinced that he has no intention of seeking help with his addictions?"

"Is my husband's behavior disruptive outside the home?"

"Does he get into fights at work or with neighbors?"

If the answers to these questions are *yes*, then you should seriously consider the possibility of leaving the relationship before it further deteriorates and before it may lead to tragic consequences.

If I am a battered wife and I have decided to leave because my life is in danger and because there is no reasonable expectation that my marriage will improve, I should develop a simple plan of action.

a. Plan to leave before another violent confrontation. Don't wait until after the next beating. It may be your last.

b. Contact your local shelter and arrange to leave as soon as there is a vacancy available. Otherwise call a friend or relative or minister and make arrangements to stay with them. If you are working and are interested in leaving permanently, you may want to move to a new apartment. Your local shelter can help you relocate.

c. Take the children with you. If you wait for another emergency situation to arise, you may not be able to leave with the children. Too many things may happen at once and you may find it necessary to run for your life. This is why it is important to plan to leave before a crisis occurs. The chances of gaining permanent custody of the children are much better if you take them with you, than if you leave them behind regardless of the reasons.

d. Be sure to take as many personal items that you can — clothing, photos, jewelry. Your departure may lead your husband to destroy the personal possessions you leave behind. Find out 'ahead of time what you are legally entitled to as far as assets go and withdraw what is legally yours from bank accounts. An angry husband may change the locks on all of the doors, remove your name from charge cards and withdraw all money from joint checking and savings accounts, leaving you and the children destitute. If however, you are unable to protect your property and financial assets, remember that your life is more important than your lifestyle. Don't compromise when it comes to a choice between them.

How the Child in Crossfire Can Get Help

If I am a child in the crossfire, I can help myself by:

a. Removing myself from the area in the home where the fighting is taking place. If a violent argument occurs while you are awake, you should leave the house and go to a neighbor's place until it is safe to return. This should be done as quietly and quickly as possible without drawing attention. If it should occur while you are asleep, either stay in your room or move to a room where there is a telephone. If the violence escalates and you need to call an ambulance or the police, you'll be able to make the call without notice.

b. Not blaming myself for the violence in the home. Each of your parents are responsible for their own behavior and for their own choices in life. Their marriage is fraught with violent confrontation because of reasons that have nothing to do with you. Chances are if you had not been born, they would still have a violent relationship. People are violent because they may have been abused by their parents or because they never learned how to disagree in a non-violent way. You should also know that there is only one underlying reason for this practice. Wife-beating and child abuse have their roots in a long worldwide history of violence against women and children. For centuries they have been regarded as the property of their husbands or fathers, which has often resulted in their maltreatment. Don't blame yourself for the violence in the home.

c. Making friends and becoming involved in school activities. Feeling good about yourself comes from within. Feelings of shame and embarrassment come from guilt. But you are not responsible for your parents' problems. You have a right to develop yourself to your fullest potential and to believe in yourself. You have the power to create your own world and your own happiness. Although it may seem like an impossibility, it is not beyond your reach. You just have to look beyond the crossfire — beyond the violence to find your peace and the power to change defeat to victory.

d. Standing on my own two feet. This means that you will not use alcohol or drugs to drown out the pain — the hurt — the constant fear of being maimed or killed or of your mother's potential murder. The nightmares — the sleepless nights — the tension — the visual fear of finding your mother brutally attacked or savagely massacred upstairs on the bathroom floor. How easy it would be to take an overdose of Mom's Valium — how appealing the crack high or the delirium from beer. They take the edge off. They create a new world. But only for a moment. You know that this is running away from life and that it does not solve your problem. It doesn't change a thing. Only you can change and you can do it, if you believe in your ability to survive against the odds.

e. Reaching out to others for friendship and guidance. When you believe in yourself, you begin to love yourself. When this happens, you are able to express an interest in others, to trust them and to confide in them. It is important to be able to tell someone special about your problems at home. Sometimes a guidance counselor at school can be very helpful. Certainly if your life is in danger, you shouldn't hesitate about getting help. If you build up a network of support, you won't have to run away from home or attempt suicide.

f. Exchanging frightening thoughts of killing my father or mother for positive thoughts where I can see him and my mom and myself hugging and embracing. Many children and young people have these kinds of "bad" thoughts. They make you toss and turn at night. They make you look long and hard in the bathroom mirror. You are frightened of what you have become and of what you might do. You struggle against such dark unmentionable thoughts. All the while these thoughts come back to haunt you. If only you could make the fighting stop! If only you could stop it forever! You are obsessed with the thought. You can't get it out of your head. This is because you give this thought a power of its own. You dwell on it too long and you chastise yourself for having it. You call yourself a bad person and you begin to believe that the violence between your parents has entered your own mind and heart.

But you can stop the thoughts. They need you to give them life. Try to block them by this simple method. Replace them as quickly as possible with a counter thought that is positive. Each time the violent thought enters your mind, replace it quickly with a positive thought. This thought can be about anything that gives you pleasure and makes you feel good. Don't leave your mind blank. That will give it room for another disturbing thought to enter. Create a bit of a competitive atmosphere — call it a battle of wits. Before you know it, you won't be able to tolerate any violent images. You have turned yourself on to positive imaging. You can begin to trust yourself again. Once you have won this battle, you will never feel insecure about yourself again. You have just replaced the darkness with light and that is a positive reflection on you.

g. Studying hard and working up to potential. It's almost impossible to study at home. You never know when the arguments will start. Your nerves are always on edge. Why not stay at the library after school? Try to get there with friends or neighbors. If you're old enough to drive, there shouldn't be a problem. Getting good grades is just another way of saying you love yourself.

h. Avoiding physical fights at school or with brothers or sisters. You have a bad temper. Sometimes you fight with your boyfriend or girlfriend and you shout and throw things around, maybe slamming doors and using four-letter words. If you're a girl you might shout back or talk back to teachers. You might let your boyfriend slap you and get away with it. You have come to expect violence as a way of life. You can't blame your parents for your behavior.

Remember you are responsible for your own choices in life and hitting someone who disagrees with you or screaming at the top of your voices is a choice you make. You can stop yourself from punching, kicking, and insulting others by admitting that you have a problem and then by doing something about it. This will probably be the most difficult challenge in your lifetime because years of witnessing abusive behavior have made their mark on you. You will have a lot of unlearning to do and it won't be easy but it can be done.

How the Batterer Can Get Help

If I am a batterer, I can help myself by resolving to change my behavior today because battering is destructive and is harmful to me, my wife, my children and my marriage. It will help to keep the following information and suggestions in mind:

a. Domestic violence has recently come to be recognized as a serious crime. It can lead to physical and psychological injury or death and imprisonment. Assaulting wives, maiming and killing children have consequences in this society. Police in some states are required to make mandatory arrests, even if they have not witnessed the alleged crime but they still need corroboration in the form of physical evidence or witnesses.

b. Accept responsibility for my behavior because it is I who is doing the assaulting. Even though your wife may be contributing to the interpersonal conflict, she is not responsible for your violent assaults. This is very difficult to admit. Your tendency is to blame your wife for your lack of control.

   You often say that she makes you angry — she gets on your nerves. You tell yourself and her that she is a bad wife and mother and that she is a failure. You are constantly denying how serious your attacks are and that they are steadily getting more and more vicious. You don't want to face your own rage. You rationalize your behavior by faulting her "nagging" or "criticizing" and yet you make no attempt to sever the relationship or get help for yourself. You make the marriage's success or failure solely her responsibility. This kind of thinking has to stop if you are serious about improving your relationship and changing things.

   The first step in the right direction is to accept responsibility for your own assaultive behavior whatever your wife says or whatever your kids do are irrelevant. Ultimately you and only you bear the responsibility for hitting, punching, choking, suffocating, killing your wife or child. No one else can share it with you. You have learned this behavior, and you can unlearn it. It is a matter of choice — your choice.

c. Find out where the nearest self-help counselling group for batterers is located and call to make an appointment. Call your local **Family Service Agency, Inc.,** or

United Way Referral now. Don't wait for another incident to occur. Don't think that things will get better without intervention.

You deserve to help yourself. It can only make your life better — make you a better person. Deep down inside you really don't like yourself. But it's hard for you to admit your feelings. You don't want anyone to know about your fears — your shortcomings. You think it's not masculine to want to be caring or gentle. You're afraid of what others might think about you. You don't want to be regarded a wimp. You want to withhold your feelings. You don't feel comfortable sharing them with others. You feel vulnerable.

This is why it is so important to pick up the phone and make the call. You will discover that you are not alone. Many men with violent tempers have similar misgivings. You will discuss common problems and give each other support, encouragement and constructive criticism. Usually a trained counselor directs the interaction of the group and keeps it on its progressive course. Staying at home alone wrapped in your cocoon of self-pity and blaming will keep you in the problem.

You need to break your self-imposed isolation, reach out for help and begin the healing process. You will learn to resolve conflict, reduce stress, communicate feelings and avoid violence. The process is not one that can be accomplished overnight. If you are looking for a shortcut, you won't find it. But be prepared for the experience of a lifetime — one that will awaken your mind and your heart, and one that will open you up to a full range of feelings and emotions. You will grow and to love yourself and understand yourself more.

How the Concerned Neighbor Can Help

If I am a concerned neighbor, I can help because I have a moral responsibility to save a victim's life (child's or adult's). The abused child and family oftentimes cannot help themselves. They are so caught up in the vicious cycle that they lack the initiative and will to reach out. This is why it is so important for neighbors to act in good faith. A great majority of mothers and fathers can learn to be good mothers and fathers, but they can't do it without the proper intervention.

Domestic violence can occur anywhere — right next door or down the street; in poor, middle-class or well-to-do-families; in rural areas, suburbs or cities. By law you cannot be prosecuted for acting in good faith. You are disturbed by the fighting and screaming. You worry about the little girl in the apartment down the hall. You lose sleep over the little boy in the house on the corner. You have heard the children cry out in pain. You have seen the welts on their bodies. Their sad eyes stay in your mind. You are torn up inside.

Be a friend. Contact local service agencies listed in your phone book, such as:

- Children's Protective Services (usually a hot-line). Don't drop the ball. Be prepared to make follow-up calls to make sure that an investigation has been done. You can call anonymously.
- Local Social Service Agency.
- Public Health Authority
- School Nurse or Counselor
- Police
- Hospital (in an emergency)

Make a commitment to keeping children safe. The problem is enormous, but you can make a difference. Children belong to the Family of Man. We are all a part of that family. There is no reason why adults can't look out for all children. Be vigilant. Be responsive. But most of all be responsible. By saving a child today, we break the cycle of violence for tomorrow's children.

National Sources of Help and Information

1. **Batterers Anonymous**, c/o Coalition for Parenting of Abuse of Women and Children, P.O. Box 29, Redlands, CA 92373.
2. **Center for Women Policy Studies**, 2000 P St., N.W., Suite 508, Washington, DC 20036, (202) 872-1770. (Information about services and programs for battered children, battered women, and men who batter is available through this center.)
3. **Childhelp USA's National Child Abuse Hotline**, (800) 4-A-CHILD.
4. **Family Service Agency, Inc.** . . . In the white pages of your phone book under "F".
5. **National Clearinghouse on Marital Rape**, Women's History Research Center, 2325 Oak St., Berkeley, CA 94708.
6. ***National Coalition against Domestic Violence**, 1500 Massachusetts Ave., N.W., Suite 35, Washington, DC 20036. (Information about programs for men who batter is available through this organization.)
   *Most states have statewide coalitions working against domestic violence which can be contacted in state capitals.
7. **National Exchange Club Foundation for the Prevention of Child Abuse**, (419) 535-3232.
8. **Shelter Aid**, (800)-333-SAFE.
9. **Parents Anonymous**, (800) 421-0353.
10. **Survivor's Network**, 18653 Ventura Blvd., #143, Tarzana, CA 91356.
11. **United Way - Crisis Line/Information and Referral** . . . In the white pages of your phone book under "U".

References

1. Harry Elmer Barnes and Negley K. Teeters, **New Horizons in Criminology.** 3rd ed., Englewood Cliffs, New Jersey: Prentice Hall, Inc., 1963:162.
2. Maria Roy and Marcia Wooding Caro, **Up from Battering.** New York: Abused Women's Aid in Crisis, Inc. 1981: 35-69.
3. Martha Jane Cocker, Patricia Petway Durret, Suart Ann Gibson, **Child Abuse and Neglect in the Backgrounds of Multiple Offenders Convicted of Crimes against the Person.** Submitted in partial fulfillment of the Degree of Master of Social Work in the College of Social Work: University of South Carolina, 1979.
4. Maria Roy, **The Abusive Partner: An Analysis of Domestic Battering.** New York: Van Nostrand Reinhold Co., 1982: 126-135.
5. Ibid., 267-276.
6. J.C. Carroll, "The Intergenerational Transmission of Family Violence: The Long-Term Effects of Aggressive Behavior". *Aggressive Behavior* 3(3), Fall 1977) : 289-299.
7. D. Miller and G. Challas, "Abused Children as Adult Parents: A Twenty-Five Year Longitudinal Study". *National Conference for Family Violence Researchers,* Durham, N.H., July 21-24, 1981: 1-11.
8. R. Emerson Dobash and Russell Dobash, **Violence against Wives.** New York: The Free Press, 1979: 152-155.
9. Maria Roy, **Battered Women: A Psychosociological Study of Domestic Violence.** New York: Van Nostrand Reinhold Co. 1977: 30.
10. Ibid., 25-44.

11. Murray A. Straus, Richard J. Gelles and Suzanne K. Steinmetz, **Behind Closed Doors**. New York: Anchor Press/Doubleday, 1980. The Family Violence Research Program at the University of New Hampshire was supported by grants from the National Institute of Mental Health (MH 27557, MHI3050 and T35 MH 15161). The sample included 2,143 completed interviews with 960 men and 1,183 women. The 2,143 families interviewed reported 1,146 had children between the ages of three and seventeen living at home. It is important to note that children under the age of three were not included in the study.

12. The study commonly referred to as the **National Study of the Incidence and Severity of Child Abuse and Neglect: Executive Summary** was supported by the National Center on Child Abuse and Neglect. The study methodology involved the collection of data on suspected incidents of child abuse and neglect occurring in a sample of 26 U.S. counties located in 10 States. The sample included urban, suburban and rural counties scattered across the nation from the East Coast to the West Coast (May 1979-April 1980). In addition, data were collected from other community institutions (e.g., schools, hospitals, police, courts) for a four-month period during the fall and winter of 1979-80. Common definitions of child abuse and neglect were used for data collection by the nearly 600 participating agencies in the 26 counties. The data collected from the sample counties were used to project national estimates of the incidence and severity of child abuse and neglect. It is the first national study of child abuse and neglect which has used common and consistent definitions at all data collection sites.

13. Murray A. Straus et al., **Behind Closed Doors**.

14. **Highlights of Official Child Neglect and Abuse Reporting (1983)**, Conducted by the American Humane Association, copyright 1985 by the American Humane Association. The report was made possible by Grant No. 90-CA-862 from the National Center on Child Abuse and Neglect, Children's Bureau, Administration on Children, Youth, and Families, Office of Human Development Services, U.S. Department of Health and Human Services. Its contents should not be construed as official policy of the National Center on Child Abuse and Neglect or any other agency of the federal government. Inquiries about the availability of data should be directed to the American Association for Protecting Children in Denver, Colorado, or to the National Center on Child Abuse and Neglect Clearinghouse in Washington, D.C. Detailed information on the methodology of the National Study may be obtained in the publication **Trends in Child Abuse and Neglect: A National Perspective**, (AHA, 1984).

15. Patsy A. Klaus and Michael R. Rand, U.S. Department of Justice Bureau of Justice Statistics **Special Report Family Violence**, Washington, D.C., April, 1984: 1-2.

16. Ibid., 5.

17. Ibid., 2-3.

18. **National Study of the Incidence and Severity of Child Abuse and Neglect: Executive Summary**. May, 1979-April, 1980.

19. Ibid., 3.

20. Ibid., 3.

21. Ibid., 2-3.

22. Maria Roy, **Battered Women**, 25-44.

23. Highlights of **Official Child Neglect** and Abuse Reporting (1983): American Humane Association, 9725 East Hempden Avenue, Denver, Colorado 80231; published in 1985.

24. Ibid., 3.

25. Ray E. Helfer and C. Henry Kempe (ed.). **The Battered Child.** Chicago and London: The University of Chicago Press, 1968: 3-16.

26. Ibid., an essay by Samuel X. Radbill: 6.

27. See note #11 above for information about the study. The citation can be found on page 5 of the study.

28. Anne H. Cohn, D.P.H., Executive Director of the National Committee For Prevention of Child Abuse authored the pamphlet, "**It Shouldn't Hurt To Be A Child.**" Chicago, Illinois, 1982 :4.

29. Edward F. Dolan, Jr. **Child Abuse.** New York: Franklin Watts, 1980: 29-30.

30. Peggy Charren and Martin W, Sandler, **Changing Channels: Living (Sensibly) with Television.** Reading, Massachusetts: Addison-Wesley Puyblishing Co., 1983: 2-3.

31. Ibid., 232-233.

32. Ray E. Helfer and C. Henry Kempe, **The Battered Child.**

33. **Highlights of Official Child Neglect and Abuse Reporting, 1983,** 2.

34. Terry Davidson, in **Battered Women: A Psychosociological Study of Domestic Violence.** New York: Van Nostrand Reinhold Company, 1977: 2-23.

35. Ibid., 20.

36. Nicole Castan, "Divers aspects de la constrainte maritale, d'apres les documents judiciaires du XVIIIe siecle, "trans. Kath Ryall. Paper presented to the American Sociological Association Convention, New York City, August 1976 :5.

37. Vincent Cronin, **Napoleon Bonaparte, An Intimate Biography.** New York: Morrow, 1972: 29.

38. Davidson, in **Battered Women,** 15.

39. Roy, **Battered Women,** such passages were translated by Quandra Prettyman Stadler into modern English and appear at the beginning of each Chapter in the book.

40. Sir William Blackstone, 1, **Commentaries on the Laws of England,** 444, 1765.

41. Miriam F. Hirsch, **Women and Violence.** New York: Van Nostrand Reinhold Company, 1981: 184.

42. Terry Davidson, **Conjugal Crime.** New York: Ballantine Books, 1978: 217.

43. R. Emerson Dobash and Russell Dobash, **Violence Against Wives: A Case Against the Patriarchy.** New York: The Free Press, 1979: 10.

44. Attorney General's Task Force on Family Violence, **Final Report.** Washington, D.C.: September, 1984 : 3.

45. Maria Roy, **Battered Women: A Psychosocialogical Study of Domestic Violence,** 40.

46. U.S. Department of Health and Human Services **Interdisciplinary Glossary on Child Abuse and Neglect: Legal, Medical, Social Work Terms.** Washington, D.C.: 1980: DHHS Publication No. (OHDS) 80-30137.

47. Robert Sadoff, M.D., transcript #07095 from the Donahue Show. Multimedia Entertainment, Inc., 1984: 9.

48. Ibid., 15.

49. Ibid., 11.

50. Lenore E. Walker, **The Battered Women.** New York: Harper Colophon Books, Harper & Row, Publishers, 1979: 46.

51. Ibid., 49-50.

52. Ibid., 53.

53. Faith McNulty, **The Burning Bed.** New York: Harcourt Brace Jovanovich, 1980: 140.

54. Ibid., 285.

55. John Monahan, **Predicting Violent Behavior.** Beverly Hills: Sage Publications, 1981: 151.

56. Ibid., 152.

57. Maria Roy, **Battered Women,** 29-30.

58. Straus, Gelles, Steinmetz, **Behind Closed Doors,** 253-266.

59. Robert J. Powers and Irwin L. Kutash, "Alcohol, Drugs, and Partner Abuse," in **The Abusive Partner,** New York : Van Nostrand Reinhold Company, 1982: 69.

60. Marcia Wooding Caro, "Free at Last" in **Up from Battering** by Maria Roy and Marcia Wooding Caro: 113-132.

61. Ibid., 119.

62. James Youniss and Jacqueling Smollar, **Adolescent Relations with Mothers, Fathers, and Friends.** Chicago: The University of Chicago Press, 1985: 99.

63. Ibid., 72, 73.

64. Maria Roy, This term was coined while conducting the study in an attempt to describe the rigidly narrow system of conflict resolution that was employed by most of the participants in the study.

65. Dr. Thomas Gordon, **P.E.T. In Action,** New York: Bantam Books, 1976: 175.

66. Dr. Haim G. Ginott, **Between Parent and Teenager.** New York: The Macmillan Company, 1969: 81-110.

67. Edward A. Charlesworth and Ronald G. Nathan, **Stress Management: A Comprehensive Guide to Wellness.** New York: Ballantine Books, 1982: 20-35.

Bibliography

Books

Bach, George R. and Wyden.The Intimate Enemy. New York: Avon Books, 1968.

Barnhill, Laurence. Clinical Approaches to Family Violence. Rockville, Md.: Aspen Systems Corp., 1982.

Bonham, Marilyn. The Laughter and Tears of Children. New York: The Macmillian Company, 1968.

Branden, Nathaniel. The Psychology of Self-Esteem. Los Angeles, California: Nash Publishing Corporation, 1969.

Charlesworth, Edward A. and Nathan, Ronald G. Stress Management: A Comprehensive Guide to Wellness. New York: Ballantine Books, 1984.

Davidson, Terry. Conjugal Crime: Understanding and Changing the Wife-Beating Pattern. New York: Ballantine Books, 1978.

Derlega, Valerian and Janda, Louis. Study Guide to Accompany Personal Adjustment. Glenview, Illinois: Scott, Foresman & Company, 1978.

Dinkmeyer, Don and McKay, Gary D. The Parent's Handbook: Systematic Training for Effective Parenting. Circle Pines, Minn.: American Guidance Service, 1982.

Dobash, Emerson and Dobash, Russell. Violence Against Wives. New York: The Free Press, 1979.

Dreikurs, Rudolf. A Parent's Guide to Child Discipline. New York: Hawthorne Books, Inc., 1970.

Erikson, Erik H. Identity Youth and Crisis. New York: W. W. Norton & Co. Inc., 1968.

Faber, Adele and Mazlish, Elaine. **Liberated Parents, Liberated Children**. New York: Avon Books, 1974.

Finkelhor, David, Gelles, Richard J., Hotalling, Gerald T., Straus, Murray A. (ed.). **The Darkside of Families: Current Family Violence Research**. Beverly Hills: Sage Publications, 1983.

Glenn, Myra C. **Campaigns Against Corporal Punishment: Prisoners, Sailors, Women**. New York: State University of New York Press, 1984.

Gondolf, Edward W. **Men Who Batter: An Integrated Approach for Stopping Wife Abuse**. Holmes Beach, Florida: Learning Publications, Inc., 1985.

Gordon, Thomas. **P.E.T. In Action**. New York: Bantam Books, 1976.

Green, Maurice (ed.), **Violence and the Family**. Boulder, Colorado: Published by Westview Press for the American Association for the Advancement of Science, 1980.

Hamblin, Robert L., Buckholdt, David, Ferritor, Daniel, Kozloff, Martin and Blackwell, Lois. **The Humanization Processes: A Social Behavioral Analysis of Children's Problems**. New York: Robert E. Krieger Publishing Company, 1978.

Hansen, James C. (ed.), **Clinical Approaches to Family Violence**. Rockville, Maryland: Aspen Systems Corporation, 1982.

Hardyck and Petrinovich. **Understanding Research in the Social Sciences**. Philadelphia: W. B. Saunders Company, 1975.

Hebb, Donald Olding. **A Textbook of Psychology**. Philadelphia: W. B. Saunders Company, 1958.

Helfer, Ray E. and Kempe, C. Henry. **The Battered Child**. Chicago: The University of Chicago Press, 1968.

Hipple, John and Cimbolic, Peter. **The Counselor and Suicidal Crisis**. Springfield, Illinois: Charles C. Thomas Publisher, 1979.

Hirsch, Miriam F. **Women and Violence**. New York: Van Nostrand Reinhold Company, 1981.

Johnson, Spencer. **One Minute For Myself**. New York: William Morrow & Company, Inc., 1985.

Johnson, Spencer. **The One Minute Father**. New York: William Morrow & Company, Inc., 1983.

Johnson, Spencer. **The One Minute Mother**. New York: William Morrow & Company, Inc., 1983.

Jenkins, Gladys Gardner, Shacter, Helen S., and Bauer, William W. **These Are Your Children**. Glenview, Illinois: Scott, Foresman & Company, 1953.

Kemmer. Elizabeth Jane. **Violence in the Family: An Annotated Bibliography**. New York: Garland Publishers, 1984.

Kempe, C. Henry and Helfer, Ray E. **Helping the Battered Child and His Family**. Philadelphia: J. B. Lippincott Company, 1972.

Layne, Lisa and Paul Sinn. **The Book of Love**. New York: Simon & Schuster, Inc., 1984.

McGovern, Cecelia. **Services to Children in Institutions**. Washington: National Conference of Catholic Charities, 1948.

McNulty, Faith. **The Burning Bed**. New York: Harcourt Brace Javanovich, 1980.

McQuade, Walter and Aikman, Ann. **Stress**. New York: Bantam Books, 1974.

Mark, Vernon H. and Ervin, Frank R. **Violence and the Brain**. New York: Harper & Row, 1970.

Missildine, W. Hugh.Your Inner Conflicts: How to Solve Them. New York: Simon & Schuster, 1974.

Monahan, John. Predicting Violence Behavior. Beverly Hills: Sage Publications, 1981.

Morris, Desmond. Intimate Behavior. New York: Random House, 1971.

Muuss, Rof E. Adolescent Behavior and Society: A Book of Readings. New York: Random House, 1971.

Myers, Gail E. and Myers, Michelle Tolela. The Dynamics of Human Communication: A Laboratory Approach. New York: McGraw-Hill Book Company, 1973.

NiCarthy, Ginny. Getting Free: A Handbook for Women in Abusive Relationships. Seattle, Washington: The Seal Press, 1982.

Ochberg, Frank M. and Soskis, David, A. (ed.). Victims of Terrorism. Boulder, Colorado: Westview Press, 1982.

Okun, Lewis. Woman Abuse: Facts Replacing Myths. Albany: State University of New York Press: 1986.

O'Neill, Nena and O'Neill, George. Shifting Gears. New York: M. Evans & Company, Inc., 1967.

Orem, R.C. (ed.). A Montessori Handbook. New York: Capricorn Books, 1966.

Pagelow, Mildred Daley. Woman-Battering: Victims and Their Experiences. Beverly Hills: Sage Publications, 1981.

Patterson, Gerald R. and Gullion, M. Elizabeth. Living with Children. Champaign, Illinois: Research Press, 1968.

Pfohl, Stephen J. Predicting Dangerousness. Lexington, Mass.: Lexington Books, 1978.

Richette, Lisa Aversa. The Throwaway Children. New York: J. B. Lippincott Company, 1969.

Rofes, Eric, (ed.). The Kids' Book of Divorce. Lexington, Mass.: The Lewis Publishing Co., 1981.

Rose, Thomas, (ed.). Violence in America. New York: Random House, 1969.

Roy, Maria and Caro, Marcia Wooding. Up from Battering. New York: AWAIC, Inc., 1981.

Roy, Maria (ed.). Battered Women: A Psychosociological Study of Domestic Violence. New York: Van Nostrand Reinhold Company, 1977.

Roy, Maria (ed.). The Abusive Partner: An Analysis of Domestic Battering. New York: Van Nostrand Reinhold Company, 1982.

Rubin, Theodore Issac. Compassion and Self-Hate. New York: David McKay Company, Inc., 1975.

Rubin, Theodore Issac. Inner Peace in an Age of Anxiety. New York: The Viking Press, 1980.

Schafer, Charles. How to Influence Children: A Handbook of Practical Parenting Skills. New York: Van Nostrand Reinhold Company, 1978.

Seixas, Judith S. and Youcha, Geraldine. Children of Alcoholism; A Survivor's Manual. New York: Crown Publishers, Inc. 1985.

E. M. Standing. Maria Montessori: Her Life and Work. California: New American Library, 1962.

Steinmetz, Suzanne K. and Straus, Murray A. Violence in the Family. New York: Harper & Row, 1974.

Straus, Murray A., Gelles, Richard J. and Steinmetz, Suzanne. Behind Closed Doors. New York: Anchor Books, 1980.

Tannen, L. That's Not What I Meant. New York: Simon & Schuster, 1982.

Tavris, Carol. **Anger: The Misunderstood Emotion.** New York: Simon & Schuster, 1982.

Walker, Lenore, E. **The Battered Woman.** New York: Harper Colophon Books, Harper & Row Publishers, 1979.

Williams, Joan M. **The Psychology of Communication.** Lexington, Mass.: Xerox Individualized Publishing, 1977.

Winder, Alvin E. and Angus, David L. **Adolescence: Contemporary Studies.** New York: American Book Company, 1968.

Wiseman, Jacqueline P. (ed.). **People as Partners.** San Francisco: Canfield Press, 1971.

Wolfgang, Marvin E. and Weiner, Neil Alan. **Criminal Violence.** Beverly Hills: Sage Publications, 1982.

Youniss, James and Smollar, Jacqueline. **Adolescent Relations with Mothers, Fathers, and Friends.** Chicago: The University of Chicago Press, 1985.

Dissertation

Fromm, Jean Karen. "**The Effects of Wife Abuse on the Children**": A dissertation presented to faculty of the Graduate School of Southern California in partial fulfillment of the requirements for the Degree, Doctor of Philosophy (Education), November, 1983.

Articles

Anagnost, Eloise: Mallory, L.; Modiglianii, K.; Yinger, K. "Children in Shelters: A Resource Guide for Family Violence Programs," available from Domestic Violence Project/Safe House, 32 N. Washington, Ypsilanti, MI.

Armstrong, Daniel, T. "Shelter Based Parenting Services; A Skill Building Process". *Children Today* March/April 15 (2): 1986.

Ayoub, C. and Jacewitz, M. "Families at Risk of Poor Parenting: A Descriptive Study of Sixty at Risk Families in a Model Prevention Program". *Child Abuse & Neglect* 6 (4) 413-422, 1982.

Elbow, Margaret. "Children of Violent Marriages: The Forgotten Victims, *"Social Casework* Oct. 63 (8): 465-471, 1982.

Gentry, C.E. "Treatment of Children in Spouse Abusive Families". *Victimology* 5 (2-4): 240-250, 1980.

Gifford, L. "Family Violence Shelters: How They Can Help Children ". *Texas Child Care Quarterly* Spring: 13-18, 1983.

Hinchey, F. and Gavelek, J.R. "Empathic Responding in Children of Battered Mothers". *Child Abuse & Nelgect* 6 (4): 395-401, 1982.

Hughes, H. "Brief Interventions with Children in a Battered Women's Shelter: A Model Preventive Program". *Family Relations J. of Applied Family & Child Studies* Oct. 31 (4): 495-502, 1982.

Hughes, H. "Changes in the Psychological Functioning of Children in a Battered Women's Shelter: A Pilot Study". *Victimology* **7** (1-4); 60-68, 1982.

Hughes, H. "Psychological Functioning of Children in a Battered Women's Shelter: A Preliminary Investigation". *American Journal of Orthopsychiatry* Jul. 53 (3): 525-531, 1983.

Janas, C. "Family Violence and Child Sexual Abuse". *Medical Hypnoanalysis* Apr. 4 (2): 68-76, 1983.

Justice, B. and Justice, R. "Clinical Approaches to Family Violence: Etiology of Physical Abuse of Children and Dynamics of Coercive Treatment". *Family Therapy Collections* **3**:1-20, 1982.

Kosky, R. "Childhood Suicidal Behaviour". *Journal of Child Psychology and Psychiatry and Allied Disciplines* Jul. 24 (3): 457-468, 1983.

Kratcoski, P. and Kratcoski, L. "The Relationship of Victimization through Child Abuse to Aggressive Delinquent Behavior". *Victimology* **7** (1-4): 199-203, 1982.

Lloyd, S.; Cate, R.; Conser, J. "Family Violence and Service Providers: Implications for Training". *Social Casework* Sept. **64** (7): 431-435, 1983.

Lystad, M. "Sexual Abuse in the Home: A Review of the Literature". *International Journal of Family Psychiatry* **3** (1): 3-31, 1982.

Pfouts, J. "Forgotten Victims of Family Violence". *Social Work* Jul. 27 (4): 367-368, 1982.

Rosenbaum, A. and O'Leary, K. "Children: The Unintended Victims of Marital Violence". *American Journal of Orthopsychiatry* Oct. **51** (4): 692-699, 1981.

Roy, M. "The Intrinsic Nature of Wifebattery". *Focus on Women: Journal of Addictions and Health* Autumn **1** (3): 168-171, 1980.

Youngerman, J. and Canino, I. "Violent Kids, Violent Parents: Family Pharmaco-therapy". *American Journal of Orthopsychiatry* Jan. **53** (1): 152-156, 1983.

Manuals

Domestic Violence Protocol Manual: For Social Wokers in Health Facilities. Prepared by the Canadian Association of Social Work Administrator's in Health Facilities. (Copies may be obtained free of charge from The National Clearing House on Family Violence, Health and Welfare Canada, Ottawa, Ontario, K1A 1B5) March, 1985.

Preventing Family Violence: A Curriculum For Adolescents. Prepared by Family Violence Curriculum Project, Boston, Massachusetts. (Resource Center for the Prevention of Family Violence and Sexual Assault, Massachusetts Department of Publich Health, 150 Tremont Street, Boston, MA 02111), 1984.

Skills for Violence-Free Relationships: Curriculum for Young People Ages 13-18. by Barrie Levy. Santa Monica, California: The Southern California Coalition on Battered Women in conjunction with The Junior League of Los Angeles, 1984.

HEALTH COMMUNICATIONS, INC.

Enterprise Center
3201 Southwest 15th Street
Deerfield Beach, FL 33442
Phone: 800-851-9100

ADULT CHILDREN OF ALCOHOLICS
Janet Woititz
Over a year on The New York Times Best Seller list,this book is the primer
on Adult Children of Alcoholics.
ISBN 0-932194-15-X   **$6.95**

STRUGGLE FOR INTIMACY
Janet Woititz
Another best seller, this book gives insightful advice on learning to love
more fully.
ISBN 0-932194-25-7   **$6.95**

DAILY AFFIRMATIONS: For Adult Children of Alcoholics
Rokelle Lerner
These positive affirmations for every day of the year paint a mental picture
of your life as you choose it to be.
ISBN 0-932194-27-3   **$6.95**

*CHOICEMAKING: For Co-dependents, Adult Children and Spirituality
Seekers* — Sharon Wegscheider-Cruse
This useful book defines the problems and solves them in a positive way.
ISBN 0-932194-26-5   **$9.95**

LEARNING TO LOVE YOURSELF: Finding Your Self-Worth
Sharon Wegscheider-Cruse
"Self-worth is a choice, not a birthright", says the author as she shows us
how we can choose positive self-esteem.
ISBN 0-932194-39-7   **$7.95**

LET GO AND GROW: Recovery for Adult Children
Robert Ackerman
An in-depth study of the different characteristics of adult children of
alcoholics with guidelines for recovery.
ISBN 0-932194-51-6   **$8.95**

LOST IN THE SHUFFLE: The Co-dependent Reality
Robert Subby
A look at the unreal rules the co-dependent lives by and the way out of the
dis-eased reality.
ISBN 0-932194-45-1   **$8.95**

New Books . . .
from Health Communications

BRADSHAW ON: THE FAMILY: A Revolutionary Way of Self-Discovery
John Bradshaw
The host of the nationally televised series of the same name shows us
how families can be healed and we as individuals can realize our full
potential.
ISBN 0-932194-54-0 $9.95

HEALING THE CHILD WITHIN: Discovery and recovery for Adult Children
of Dysfunctional Families — Charles Whitfield
Dr. Whitfield defines, describes and discovers how we can reach our
Child Within to heal and nurture our woundedness.
ISBN 0-932194-40-0 $8.95

WHISKY'S SONG: An Explicit Story of Surviving in an Alcoholic Home
Mitzi Chandler
A beautiful but brutal story of growing up where violence and neglect are
everyday occurrences conveys a positive message of survival and love.
ISBN 0-932194-42-7 $6.95

New Books on Spiritual Recovery . . .
from Health Communications

THE JOURNEY WITHIN: A Spiritual Path to Recovery
Ruth Fishel
This book will lead you from your dysfunctional beginnings to the place
within where renewal occurs.
ISBN 0-932194-41-9 $8.95

LEARNING TO LIVE IN THE NOW: 6-Week Personal Plan To Recovery
Ruth Fishel
The author gently introduces you to the valuable healing tools of
meditation, positive creative visualization and affirmations.
ISBN 0-932194-62-1 $7.95

GENESIS: Spirituality in Recovery for Co-dependents
by Julie D. Bowden and Herbert L. Gravitz
A self-help spiritual program for adult children of trauma, an in-depth
look at "turning it over" and "letting go".
ISBN 0-932194-56-7 $6.95

GIFTS FOR PERSONAL GROWTH AND RECOVERY
Wayne Kritsberg
Gifts for healing which include journal writing, breathing, positioning and
meditation.
ISBN 0-932194-60-5 $6.95

Books from . . .
Health Communications

THIRTY-TWO ELEPHANT REMINDERS: A Book of Healthy Rules
Mary M. McKee
Concise advice by 32 wise elephants whose wit and good humor will also
be appearing in a 12-step calendar and greeting cards.
ISBN 0-932194-59-1   **$3.95**

BREAKING THE CYCLE OF ADDICTION: For Adult Children of Alcoholics
Patricia O'Gorman and Philip Oliver-Diaz
For parents who were raised in addicted families, this guide teaches you
about Breaking the Cycle of Addiction from *your* parents to your children.
Must reading for any parent.
ISBN 0-932194-37-0   **$8.95**

AFTER THE TEARS: Reclaiming The Personal Losses of Childhood
Jane Middelton-Moz and Lorie Dwinnel
Your lost childhood must be grieved in order for you to recapture your
self-worth and enjoyment of life. This book will show you how.
ISBN 0-932194-36-2   **$7.95**

ADULT CHILDREN OF ALCOHOLICS SYNDROME: From Discovery to Recovery
Wayne Kritsberg
Through the Family Integration System and foundations for healing the
wounds of an alcoholic-influenced childhood are laid in this important
book.
ISBN 0-932194-30-3   **$7.95**

OTHERWISE PERFECT: People and Their Problems with Weight
Mary S. Stuart and Lynnzy Orr
This book deals with all the varieties of eating disorders, from anorexia to
obesity, and how to cope sensibly and successfully.
ISBN 0-932194-57-5   **$7.95**

Orders must be prepaid by check, money order, MasterCard or Visa.
Purchase orders from agencies accepted (attach P.O. documentation)
for billing. Net 30 days.

Minimum shipping/handling — $1.25 for orders less than $25. For
orders over $25, add 5% of total for shipping and handling. Florida
residents add 5% sales tax.